I-WE

IMAGINE WISDOM EDUCATION

By Satyanna Chris Luken

Dedicated to my son and Angel:
Christofer
June 3rd, 2004 - May 5th, 2008

THIS BOOK IS AN OVERVIEW OF THE I-WE EDUCATIONAL MODEL.
THERE WILL BE FOLLOW-UP BOOKS, OUTLINING PROPRIETARY PORTIONS OF
THE I-WE EDUCATIONAL MODEL

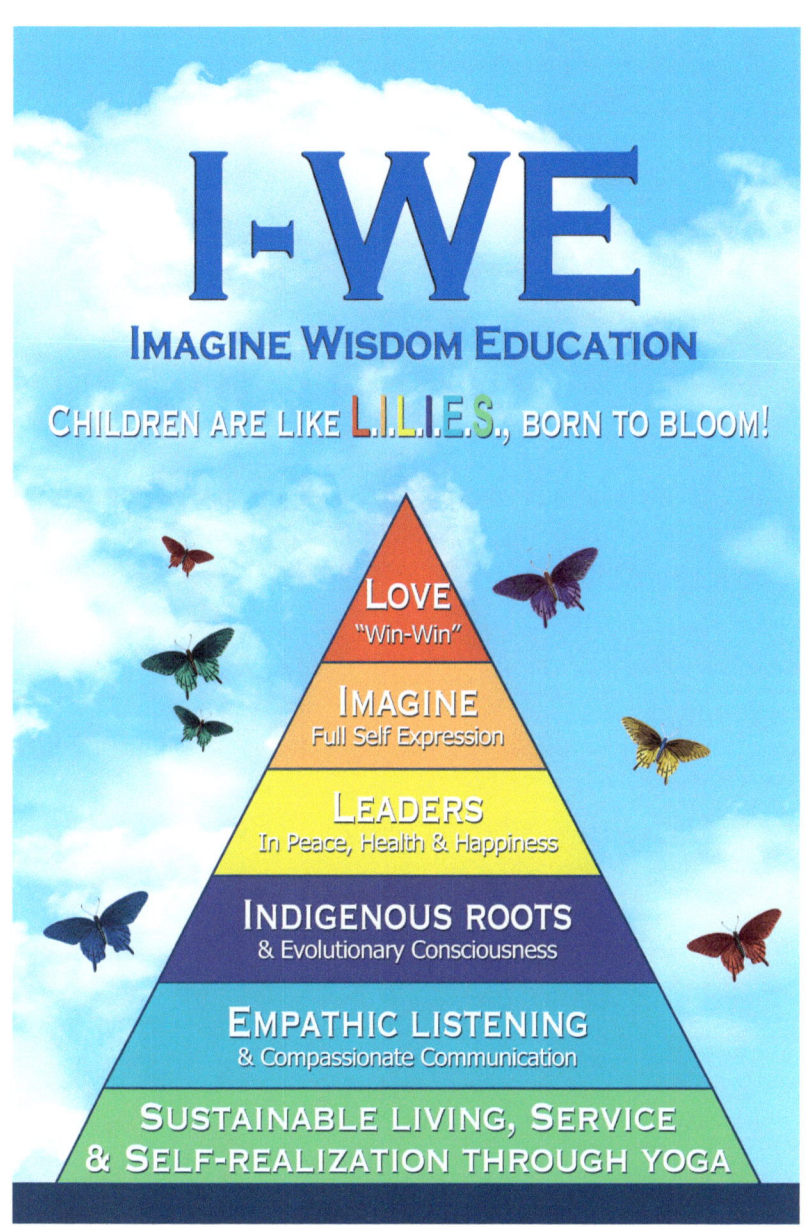

I-WE
Imagine Wisdom Education

Printed in the United States by:
CreateSpace

Copyright © 2014 by Satyanna Chris Luken (Formerly known as Anna Krajec)

All rights reserved. No part of this book may be used or reproduced in any manner whatsoever, including Internet usage, without written permission from the Author, except in case of brief quotations embodied in critical articles and reviews.

First Edition

Book Cover Designed by:
Danny Fitch
www.behance.net/dany_fitch

ISBN-13:
978-0615994604
(I-WE-Imagine Wisdom Education)
ISBN-10:
0615994601

TABLE OF CONTENTS

FOREWORD………………………………………........	11
ENDORSEMENTS……………………………,…	13
INTRODUCTION………………………………,,,,…	21
HOW I-WE CAME TO BE……………………………,…	27
"The Start of Something New"……………………	33
Early Parenting - Early Education………………...	35
Illness and Loss, and Legacy………………….......	37
PEARLS OF WISDOM COLLECTED THROUGHOUT MY TEACHING YEARS......................	41
OUR PUBLIC EDUCATION AND BEYOND………….	45
Unschooling and hackschooling………………….	51
The Measure of Success……………………........	55
THE VISION OF I-WE………………………………….	59
WHO CAN START AN I-WE SCHOOL?........................	63
How to Legally Unschool Your Children..........................	65
THE MISSION OF I-WE…………………………………	67
THE 6 PILLARS OF I-WE'S STARGAZER LILIES…...	73
1. **L**ove - A 'Win-Win' Experience for All……….	75
2. **I**magine… Full Self-Expression………………...	77
3. **L**eaders in Peace, Health and Happinesss……...	79
4. **I**ndigenous Roots & Evolutionary Consciousness…………………………………....	83
5. **E**mpathic Listening & Compassionate Communication…………….	85
6. **S**ustainable Living, **S**ervice and Self-Realization through Yoga………………….	87
SUSTAINABLE LIVING - GREEN VALENTINES,……	91
THE CLASSROOM - PREPARED ENVIRONMENT….	95
PLAY AREA……………………………………………...	107
OUR LAGUNA BEACH TEAM ………………………	115
Visionary………………………………………...	115
Our Community Leaders and I-WE Teachers….....	116
ONGOING I-WE COMMUNITY…………………………	123
Eighteen Leaders from our Community Share Their Passions……………………………………….	125
1. Mathematics for the Children of the Future…...	127
2. Gardening and Cooking with Children……….	133

3. The New Path for Early Childhood Education..	137
4. Public Speaking; From Painful to Powerful.....	139
5. The 'Living Your Gifts' Girls' Workshop......,.	147
6. Waking Up the Women of the World!.............	154
7. Children as Canvasses………………………...	157
8. Music and Creativity in the Classroom…….....	159
9. Healing with Crystals and Fashion....................	165
10. Electrical Engineering (EE) as a Career………	168
11. My Horse Journey…………………………….	171
12. Kianti's Natural Outdoor Fitness Training Class for Early Teens………………...	175
13. Education Transformations …………………...	178
14. Learning and Being our Authentic Selves…….	185
15. Personal Empowerment Principles……….…....	189
16. A Little Child Shall Lead Them ……………...	193
17. HeartThread and Healing……………………...	197
18. Where Giving Back Comes Before Art…….....	201
ACKNOWLEDGEMENTS………………………....	203
DEEP GRATITUDE…………………………….…..	204
CALLS TO ACTION………………………………...	207
NOTE FROM THE AUTHOR……………………....	210
THE CHILDREN OF THE FUTURE THANK YOU!…...	213
MESSAGES FROM CHRISTOFER ☺………………...	217
DEDICATION………………………………………..	218
ABOUT THE AUTHOR……………………………...	219

From full body experience to art on paper

FOREWORD

"It is the child who makes the man, and no man exists who was not made by the child he once was." This powerful quote from Maria Montessori a century ago forever changed the way we educate children. Satyanna Chris Luken (formerly known as Anna Krajec) is following in her footsteps to advocate a learning environment that echoes Montessori's quote above. I am delighted to have an opportunity to write an introduction to her book titled "*I-WE Imagine Wisdom Education*", and wish her every success.

I have known Satyanna for nearly twenty years. She trained, and later came to work, at the Montessori Institute where I am an instructor. We have always kept in touch through all her callings and experiments. Anna has taken her experiences from teaching, her quest for spiritual knowledge and most importantly, motherhood, and paved her way into creating an educational theory that is child centered; where a child is able to create his learning environment and develop his own curriculum according to his interests, by partnering with the community that surrounds him. She is inviting us to join her in creating this dynamic learning environment in our communities and revolutionize the prevailing mainstream educational methods. It is commendable that she acknowledges all the educational methods that she has learned from and incorporated into her educational theory, thus giving them the respect they deserve. If you are a parent or a community leader I urge you to listen to what she has to say.

Deepa Somasundaram
Director/Administrator and Montessori Teacher Trainer
Montessori School of Laguna Beach, CA

**This photo was taken by
Larisa Stow, a dear friend of mine
Who also inspired the title text:
Children are like LILIES, *Born to Bloom*
From her very special song
Born to Bloom!**

ENDORSEMENTS

(Satyanna Chris Luken was formerly known as Anna Krajec)

"In my lifetime of teaching and healing work, few have touched me the way Anna has. She has a passion and dedication to children, this planet, and us adults; who ultimately determine the course for those children on this planet.
This book is her gift to us. All who find their way onto its pages will find inspiration and guidance that will serve them well, and therefore serve us all."
Heather George - www.TheLotusWay.org

One of our wonderful I-WE moms, Amy, contributed an important point for my first book titled '*ABC of Conscious Parenting – Agreements Before (and After) Conceiving.*' Education goes way beyond what public schools can provide or enforce. Education must include what we put in our bodies, such as our food choices, or the technology and media we allow our children to be exposed to:

"Concurrent to adopting the holding technique, at Satyanna's suggestion we began journaling everything Jasper ate, and quickly found a correlation between sugar and tantrums. We're a vegetarian household and really quite healthy, so we never considered the small amount of sugar in his diet to be a factor. We found out, however, that when he would eat sugar when already having a 'tantrum trigger' kind of day, it would be a combustible combination. Lastly, we completely eliminated any technology near bedtime. He does not watch TV or listen to the radio when he wakes up or near bedtime, and we've found this elimination to be really helpful in easing into our daily patterns without distractions or tantrums. Jasper's back to his pre-monster self; he's a loving, curious, active and sometimes cranky two-and-a-half-year-old!"
Amy - Laguna Beach, CA

The endorsement that follows is from one of my current clients, Kortney, who is the amazing mother to Mia (7) and Quinn (5). Kortney embodies the essence of my ideal client; trusting my recommendations, and being willing to implement them, even when the task is difficult (such as taking away screen time and replacing it with enriching activities), knowing there will be benefits later. I am so grateful for the opportunity to make a difference in their lives.

"We started working with Satyanna six months ago. I originally brought her into our home to teach French and do yoga with my then seven-year-old daughter and four-year-old son. At the time my son was experiencing some sensory issues, anxiety, and difficulty attending to task.

We have received so much more than I initially signed up for. My son has learned to self-regulate his body and decrease his anxiety through meditation, songs, and yoga. She started working with him three days a week and he now knows his numbers, letters, and can read the first set of the "Bob" books, My son can easily attend a lesson up to 30-45 minutes now. My daughter has shifted as well, she now journals about her feelings. She has more of a leadership role at school. She is reading, writing and speaking French.

I believe Satyanna was put on this earth to heal, teach, and guide adults and children how to love more, learn more, and to reconnect with the earth and what really matters.

Satyanna has an amazing ability of connecting with humans, making you feel loved, making you feel deserving of good things. She works on an extraordinary level, which is different from most people. Through little suggestions of how to tweak our lifestyle and our home environment, we have turned our home and our children's minds around. Within a month of removing the TV's out of the home, my son began to reconnect with his imagination. He is more focused, more articulate, and more connected. I cannot say enough about Sataynna. Simply put, she has been a huge blessing and a true gift to my family and me!"
Kortney Riley, Laguna Beach, CA

"The I-WE educational model allows children to be educated in the way their spirit needs to be educated, instead of the way society is telling us to educate. If I had known about this model when my children were little I would have chosen this way of learning. This is a brilliant teaching model. It allows for our children to have a great education, as well as a future of happiness."
Susan Hough
Co-Founder of Living Your Gifts
and Youth Project Coordinator of Wisdom Spring, Inc.

"I feel so blessed to count Satyanna as one of my dearest friends. We first met when my youngest son (then, age 3, now, nearly 19) was a student in her class at Anneliese's Academy in Laguna Beach, CA. Regrettably, I had to move both of my sons from Anneliese's, where they were blossoming and excelling, to the public school system. While we lived in a "good" district, my sons both struggled through school, hating the entire experience and barely getting through it. Sadly, this is the experience today for many children. Having been exposed to a superior educational model at Anneliese's, I knew that learning didn't have to be drudgery; it could be magical and fun! Satyanna also knows this to be true, and has combined the best aspects of several alternative educational models to create a brilliant new model.

Satyanna has a contagious passion for what she loves, and thankfully, children are one of her greatest passions. She doesn't just see herself as their teacher, but understands that they also have something to teach us. She truly understands that our children are our future, and is committed to educating them holistically, addressing the whole person, because we are all more than just the sum of our parts, and we all do better when all parts of ourselves and our lives are in balance. Satyanna is a visionary, and I am proud to play whatever part I can in helping bring her vision for the I-WE educational model to fruition. It is long overdue."
Karene Cargill
Co-Founder of We Arts Giving Hope Foundation

"Many parents never recover from the heartbreaking loss of a child. Satyanna faced that difficult journey and returned with another precious gift: I-WE Imagine Wisdom Education, a wonderful book about an evolutionary educational model. Satyanna provides insightful guidance for those wishing to take the education of their children into their own hands, while growing a worldwide community of like-minded parents and educators. Read this inspirational book and empower your children!"

- Leonard Szymczak, MSW, LCSW,
  author of *The Roadmap Home: Your GPS to Inner Peace*

Satyanna's First Book:
ABC of Conscious Parenting:
Agreements Before Conceiving!

Our Angel caring for our garden

Planting seeds for I-WE ☺

Growing our own organic food and connecting with Nature in all ways, is a big part of our I-WE mixed ages community

"There is a road in the hearts of all of us,
hidden and seldom traveled,
which leads to an unknown secret place.

The old people came literally to love the soil,
and they sat or reclined on the ground
with a feeling of being close to a mothering power.

Their teepees were built upon the earth
and their altars were made of earth.

The soul was soothing, strengthening,
cleansing and healing.

That is why the old Indian still sits upon the earth
instead of propping himself up and
away from its life giving forces.

For him, to sit or lie upon the ground is to be able to
think more deeply
and to feel more keenly.

He can see more clearly into the mysteries of life and
come closer in kinship to other lives about him."

-Chief Luther Standing Bear

**Our beloved community elders
sharing their passion for gardening with the youth**

**And their love for the earth,
with our children**

INTRODUCTION

> *"It is, in fact, nothing short of a miracle that the modern methods of instruction have not yet entirely strangled the holy curiosity of inquiry; for this delicate little plant aside from stimulation, stands mainly in need of freedom. Without this it goes to wreck and ruin without fail."*
> **-Albert Einstein**

Growing up as a child in France, my world completely fell apart at the age of thirteen. The one part of my life that was easy, stable and somewhat predictable had become confusing and overwhelming. I was a good student and did not dislike math until a teacher, who was unable to teach this subject effectively, introduced algebra to our class. For the first time ever I felt lost and stupid. As a result, my grades and my self-esteem plummeted. I began to question my ability to think and to reason, and worried that I might not be able to survive in this world.

Having been raised bilingual (my family is from Holland), I felt bright and always capable of overcoming difficult situations, such as growing up in an unstable home environment, and losing my mother at the young age of five. My ability to be smart and resourceful was the one thing I counted on in order to feel safe in the world. After I couldn't make sense of what was being taught in my algebra class, I lost my self-confidence. It suddenly felt like a rug had been pulled out from under me, and that my survival was threatened.

> *"Study without desire spoils the memory, and it retains nothing that it takes in."*
> **-Leonardo Da Vinci**

Like many children in middle school do, I fell off the 'education train.' Due to the large class sizes, the multiple subjects taught by different teachers and the lack of communication between them, no one wondered what was causing the downward spiral in all of my grades. I don't blame my life falling apart at that time solely on that experience with algebra. However, I am aware that for me, it was the "straw that broke the camel's back."

> "One looks back with appreciation to the brilliant teachers, but with gratitude to those who touched our human feelings. The curriculum is so much necessary raw material, but warmth is the vital element for the growing plant and for the soul of the child."
> -Carl Gustav Jung

As a consequence, I quickly went from being a confident 'A' student to being told that I needed to repeat 8th grade. I never once thought to question my teacher's ability to teach when I couldn't understand the new math concepts. I just felt inadequate and thought I was dumb. And, because of that belief, I threw away my dream of becoming a school counselor, which would have required me to get a bachelor's degree. Instead I decided to attend a vocational program in business and received my degree two years later.

> "I'm a visual thinker, really bad at algebra. There are others that are a pattern thinker. These are the music and math minds. They think in patterns instead of pictures. Then there's another type that's not a visual thinker at all, and they're the ones that memorize all of the sports statistics, all of the weather statistics."
> -Dr. Temple Grandin

Does this sound familiar to you? Did anything like this happen to you or someone you love? Have you heard of others who were stopped in their forward movement by certain subjects at school? For example, did you or did someone you know struggle with spelling? So many brilliant leaders in our world were labeled dyslexic and made to feel dumb in school.

Just to name a few of these outstanding Scientists, Inventors, Artists Entrepreneurs, Performers, Physicians and Political Leaders:

- Albert Einstein   - Agatha Christie   - John Lennon
- Sir Richard Branson   - Sir Isaac Newton   - Whoopi Goldberg
- Thomas Jefferson   - Ansel Adams   - Dame Anita Roddick
- Leonardo Da Vinci   - Charles Schwab   - Pablo Picasso
- Nelson Rockefeller   - Walt Disney   - John Kennedy

Here is a link to a video of an interview with **Sir Richard Branson**, founder of Virgin Group, on TED:
http://www.youtube.com/watch?v=3XQcdVp9sls

> *"The only thing that interferes with my learning is my education."*
> **-Albert Einstein**

As a teacher and educator for over seventeen years, I have seen so many children discouraged and broken down by our outdated educational system. I routinely witnessed how the American 'cookie cutter' curriculum failed to address not only the learning needs of individual children, but also the development of the whole (physical, emotional, spiritual, imaginative, and service oriented) child. I have heard many stories over the years and dreams put on hold or never pursued.

On our website, you can see an animated video narrated by Sir Kenneth Robinson, and the video "Animal School." Both reflect my sentiments about our public education system:
http://imaginewisdomeducation-I-WE.org/INSPIRATIONS.html

Although it had been my passion and dream to work with children, I was distraught from my own experience as a student and disillusioned by a system that I did not want to support. After I received my business degree, my father sent me to the United States as an exchange student to learn English. I completed my twelfth grade with honors, even though I came without speaking or understanding the language at all. Twelfth grade in the U,S. felt easier than ninth grade in France, even with the language handicap, because the multiple-choice questions in America were far simpler than the essay questions I was accustomed to in French schools.
During that year abroad, I fell in love with America and decided to stay. I felt anything was possible here. It was the spirit of America that won my heart. I roamed around the streets, wondering what I should do with my life. I was offered a position by a family in Manhattan, as a live-in babysitter, to teach French to their young child. I survived a few more years by tutoring, babysitting, teaching French, waitressing and doing odd secretarial jobs.

> *"If I can make it there*
> *I'll make it anywhere*
> *It's up to you*
> *New York, New York"*
> **-Frank Sinatra**

While in New York, I spent all my free time taking photographs of this spectacular city. Taking photographs had been a passion of mine since I was fourteen. I had developed the habit of documenting every aspect of my life since that young age. Additionally, as soon as I saved enough money, I would travel every chance I had. My soul deeply longed for new territories and cultural experiences. I believe that while traveling, I learned more about myself, others, and life itself, than if I had stayed to pursue a bachelor's degree in France. This passion for taking pictures eventually led me to enroll in the New York Institute of Photography, where I later received my degree as a professional photographer.

> *"Do not train a child to learn by force or harshness; but direct them to it by what amuses their minds, so that you may be better able to discover with accuracy the peculiar bent of the genius of each."*
> **-John F. Kennedy**

I moved to Hollywood and became a photographer in the music industry. Soon my talent was recognized and my photographs were published in various magazines, both in the U.S. and in Europe. While I enjoyed that and got to photograph my all-time favorite musicians, such as David Bowie, Neil Young, Pink Floyd and Robert Plant.

> *"Very many people go through their whole lives having no real sense of what their talents may be, or if they have any to speak of."*
> **-Sir Ken Robinson**

I felt somewhat unfulfilled, as if I was not doing what I came to this world to do. In my quiet moments, I remember searching for my purpose. I wondered why I was alive at this time on this planet, and what I was really meant to do with my life.

Around age 27, I felt my desire to work with children become a driving force again. I had 'lived,' I had grown as a person, and possibly even became the person I was meant to be. It was time for me to find a way to work with children, down the 'path less traveled,' outside of the public education system. I decided to leave the glamorous Hollywood life, to begin my life anew, in Laguna Beach, CA.

Samples from my published portfolio

From photography to I-WE

HOW I-WE CAME TO BE

I found a private one-year certification program and enrolled at the Montessori School in Laguna Beach. This program would allow me to teach children ages 2-5, within a year of focused studies. During my in-depth training, the founder of this great educational model, Maria Montessori became my 'she-hero.' Many years later, I am still deeply moved and inspired by her contribution to education and to society.

I received my early education units within a few months, which allowed me to work as an assistant right away. During my training I was impressed by the depth and precision of each lesson. I began to truly understand **Maria Montessori's** description of the Teacher's Job:

> *"To assist a child we must provide him with an environment, which will enable him to develop freely… The environment must be rich in motives, which lend interest to activity and invite the child to conduct his own experiences… Character formation cannot be taught, it comes from experience and not from explanation…"*

During this time of preparation, I realized the importance of the teacher/student relationship, as well as the prepared environment. Maria Montessori observed how children learned to speak, by absorbing the language spoken around them, not because they were taught. She called this stage of development, the Absorbent Mind.

For this reason, the optimal time to introduce a second language is before the age of six. During this remarkable period, the child learns simply and effortlessly by absorbing everything in its environment. It is therefore essential for children to begin their education long before Kindergarten.

The adult, according to **Maria Montessori,** *is to be an inspiration for the child's actions, a kind of open book wherein a child can learn how to direct his own movements.*

> *"But, an adult, if he is to afford proper guidance, must always be calm and act slowly so that the child who is watching him can clearly see his actions in all their particulars."*

It became clear to me why the environment needs to be prepared carefully; why it must be filled with beauty and surrounded with Sensorial and Practical activities that ignite the child's natural desire to engage and learn. That is when, my journey to create those optimum conditions for the young child to bloom into, began.

Over the years, I have continued to work closely with the director of the Laguna Beach Montessori School, Deepa Somasundaram, who would occasionally call me when she needed assistance in the classroom. In addition, I have had the privilege of sharing my vision of the I-WE model with this extraordinary teacher and administrator. Her commitment to providing the children with an exceptional Montessori education resulted in her implementing activities such as yoga, gardening and foreign languages in her curriculum.

For more information about this wonderful Montessori school:
http://lagunabeachmontessori.com

> *"I think that it is not exaggerated to say that no other educational system in the world gives such a central role to the arts as the **Waldorf School Movement**. There is not a subject taught that does not have an artistic aspect. Even mathematics is presented in an artistic fashion and related via dance, movement or drawing to the child as a whole. Steiner's system of education is built on the premise that art is an integral part of human endeavors."*
> -**Konrad Oberhuber** - Harvard Fine Art Professor

I fell in love with the creative, artistic and enchanting characteristics of the Waldorf educational model after accepting a better teaching position in a local Waldorf inspired school. Although I was trained as a Montessori teacher and while still a firm believer in the model, I was thrilled to work in this exquisite school.

I got to teach French to students, grades first through sixth, in addition to a morning class with preschoolers, where I had complete freedom to teach with my Montessori materials.

The school was named after its founder, Anneliese, who had come from Germany in 1968. It was filled with *beauty* and warmth. I emphasize the word ***beauty*** because this is also something that Maria Montessori believed: *"The child should live in an environment of **beauty**."*

The enchanting setting provided an eco-friendly environment, where gardening was taught and the respectful treatment of resident animals was promoted. We had chickens, pigs, llamas, bunnies and peacocks running around the property. Anneliese cooked meals with the children and spoke German to them. She told stories, used puppets and let the children spend a lot of free time in her lush colorful gardens. They played with mud and had imaginary encounters with the gnomes and fairies.

For more information about this wonderful school you can go to: **www.Annelieseschool.com**

After my sixth year of full time teaching, I got pregnant with my son. Anneliese offered me a position co-teaching a 1st grade class part-time, which allowed me to take nursing breaks and support my co-parenting schedule.

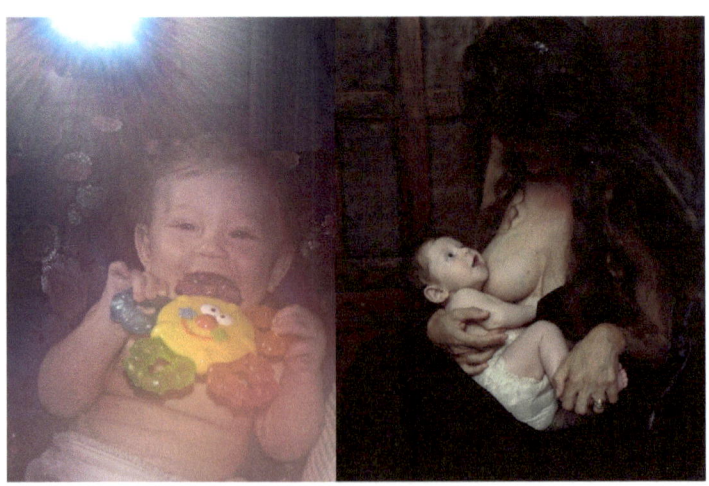

**Pregnancy and Nursing my only child
have been my most precious gifts!**

**Teaching French was a "Win-Win" activity
I could enjoy with Christofer which,
helped supplement our household income**

Bilingual parents can offer such programs

"The Start of Something New"

"And the day came when the risk to remain tight in a bud was more painful than the risk it took to blossom."
-**Anais Nin**

During my seven years working at Anneliese's, I was driven to create a program for children filled with different subjects than those I could teach in school. In my early twenties, I was fortunate to experience a workshop called Omega, which altered the course of my life. Since that time, I felt inspired to bring that kind of *mind and heart* opening experience to the youths. It was something I felt the children would really be excited about, and yet it was filled with deep wisdom.

On the other hand, I witnessed parents stressed and exhausted, overwhelmed by the demands of everyday life. I realized they needed a break to rest and reconnect with each other so they could have love and energy to give to their children. As I watched the strong ripple effect the stress was having on the entire community, I decided to create a twenty-four hour program that could support both the parents and the children.

The program was for children ages 7-12 and was called Genius Connection Playshops. Sometimes we would offer an "Occasion" for younger children, not lasting quite as long. The children were dropped off on Fridays around 4:00 pm. We would walk to the beach to do a sunset yoga class and come back to the house to cook a meal together. Then, we would sit around the fireplace and introduce our theme for the "Occasion." For example: In a Native American theme, an elder would facilitate a discussion in a circle with the children, using a 'Talking Stick' (a stick, or other chosen object, is passed from child to child as they speak). Only the person holding the stick is allowed to speak during that time, while every other member must listen closely to the words being spoken, thus encouraging speaking along with listening skills. Children would fall asleep in their sleeping bags, listening to a guided mediation. The next morning, we would make dream catchers, after preparing and drinking our own smoothies.

We offered Playshops, with topics such as Gratitude, Photography, Peaceful Leadership and Healthy Cooking:

I-WE seeds were germinating!

Sustainable Living Values and Compassionate Communication were an integral part of all the programs. Children thrived in these gatherings and the parents were grateful. I realized how much I loved teaching eclectic and enriching programs to the community. (Teaching 'out of the box' is what I always enjoyed doing the most!)

Early Parenting - Early Education

When my son, Christofer, was ten months old, I realized I wanted to become a full-time mother and stopped working at the school altogether. When he turned two, it became clear to me that I couldn't give him everything he needed for his optimum personal and educational development. Even though I spoke French to him and had set up a mini-Montessori classroom in our little house, we had no garden or room for animals. I wanted Christofer to enjoy a magical school setting in Nature, with little ones his age to play with, and no mommy around. I was looking for that perfect place when...

Illness and Loss, and Legacy

At the young age of two and half, Christofer was diagnosed with an inoperable brain tumor, and eventually lost his life to it, just before his 4th birthday. He inspired such a movement of unconditional love during his final months, which took on a life of its own, deeply touching the hearts of the entire community.

The gratitude I felt carried me through this devastating time and beyond this tremendous loss. I was so moved by the incredible financial, spiritual and emotional support we received, that I wanted to give something back. I am eternally thankful for the gifts of motherhood and community, which Christofer brought into my life.

Because I could no longer 'mother' him, I opened our home to the children of Laguna Beach and transferred that nurturing energy to support the parents who had been so good to us. This is how the 'Genius Connection Playshops' grew into 'Lilies' and evolved into the I-WE program you are reading about today. Christofer is now guiding me to share my love with the children of the world…

PEARLS OF WISDOM COLLECTED THROUGHOUT MY TEACHING YEARS

Throughout my career as a teacher, I learned about some of the different philosophies being taught to children in both the public and private sectors. While I observed each organization teaching their particular curriculum to the children, I was thankful for the unique gifts offered by these different programs. However, I recognized some of the constraints inherent in using such exclusive curriculums. In my opinion, these isolated methods were missing vital elements, which prevented them from being able to address the changing needs of all students. For this reason, I decided to become one of the pioneers who explored new ways to help shift the paradigm in education.

I began to question these 'complete' models of education, such as the Montessori and Waldorf Methods, along with approaches such as Orff Schulwerk and Reggio Emilia. While teaching with Montessori materials at Anneliese's, which was a Waldorf inspired school, I noticed two important things:

First, I saw the children were drawn to these seemingly different models, depending on where they were in their personal stage of development.

Second, the children's choices were greatly influenced by the affinities they developed in their new school environment. Being surrounded by 'little people' their own age became much more exciting to imitate than the family of origin, which had been their primary role model. Many children would become enamored with special classmates they idolized, thus wanting to mirror everything that fabulous child did.

For example, a typical three-year-old 'Waldorf child' who, in the beginning of the year, was mostly interested in play, became practically obsessed six months later, with wanting to read books. This made him pay attention to the letter sounds (in all the fun ways we explored them during our morning circle, with songs and games) and even ask for "teaching moments."

On the other hand, a typical 'Montessori child' who started the year eager to learn "table work" and model 'practical life' activities, became fascinated with dressing up and pretend-play because his or her best friend excelled at it.

Another educational experience that deeply impacted my life as both a student and an educator was my practice of yoga and meditation. As a lifelong 'seeker,' I was first introduced to it when I lived in New York and through regular practice, experienced many powerful changes in my personal life.

This is the reason I decided to implement these empowering tools in my work with children. I noticed the students were calmer and more focused immediately after our practice. It was exciting to see how the children developed a greater sense of self-confidence and flexibility in their body, mind and spirit, through their experience with Yoga. Some aspects of this extraordinary body of work proved to be particularly transformative for the special needs children.

On another note, while I was on the business track during my high school years, I realized those skills could have been learned 'in the field,' while apprenticing with an actual business. Since things are changing so rapidly in the world, I feel it is even more important for us to provide a valuable and enriching education for our youth to help them prepare for the challenges that lie ahead in their future.

During the Genius Connection Playshops, I invited community leaders to come teach their crafts to the children instead of the typical trained teachers they were accustomed to in school. By integrating various elements from these previously known as stand-alone programs, an amazing synergy was created. Children thrived in our special 'Occasions' when all these elements came together in this experimental approach.

For example, when the 'Occasion' was to learn about and celebrate Native American Teachings, our Elder, Linda Crow, came with a big drum to share her Wisdom and songs with the children. She brought scarves for the children to cover themselves with while circling the drum, pretending they embodied various animals. Children, who did not usually participate in such performing art activities, came out of their shells and became alive in a whole new way.

**We found all ages really enjoyed the Drum
& Native American Teachings**

Our philosophy of education has emerged from the ancient wisdom of indigenous teachings and the evolutionary ideas in developed in the Genius Connection Playshops. Our unique contribution provides children with a dynamic and vibrant I-WE model that includes this broad spectrum of knowledge in a relevant and synergistic way.

Through my work in developing the I-WE model, the work of Maria Montessori has been one of my greatest sources of wisdom and inspiration. It has given me the courage and the strength to honor my experiences in education as both a student and an educator and incorporate them more fully into this I-WE curriculum. I feel this model is a natural evolution of Maria Montessori's vision, and that she would fully support our growth and expansion in the global community.

OUR PUBLIC EDUCATION AND BEYOND

"We are shut up in schools and college recitation rooms for ten or fifteen years, and come out at last with a belly-full of words and do not know a thing. The things taught in schools and colleges are not an education, but the means of education."
-Ralph Waldo Emerson

The economic demands during which time public education was created required teachers to deliver reading, writing, and math fundamentals to a previously illiterate class of people, in order to create an industrial workforce.

According to **Sir Ken Robinson** in *The Element: How finding your passion changes everything* "*Public schools were not only created in the interests of industrialism—they were created in the image of industrialism. In many ways, they reflect the factory culture they were designed to support. This is especially true in high schools, where school systems base education on the principles of the assembly line and the efficient division of labor. Schools divide the curriculum into specialist segments: some teachers install math in the students, and others install history. They arrange the day into standard units of time, marked out by the ringing of bells, much like a factory announcing the beginning of the workday and the end of breaks. Students are educated in batches, according to age, as if the most important thing they have in common is their date of manufacture. They are given standardized tests at set points and compared with each other before being sent out onto the market. I realize this isn't an exact analogy and that it ignores many of the subtleties of the system, but it is close enough.*"

Education innovator **Sugata Mitra**, who received the $1 million TED prize stated in his TED talk *Kids can teach themselves*: "The Victorians created a global computer made up of people... A bureaucratic administrative machine... In order to keep it running, you need lots and lots of people. They must be identical to each other... So they created a system, called school, to make parts [for this human computer]. They must have good handwriting, they must be able to read, and they must be able to add, subtract and do division... But these skills aren't as necessary with the advent of computers. It's quite fashionable to say the education system is broken, but It's not. It's wonderfully constructed - it's just that we don't need it anymore. It's out-dated."

> *"Education can be stifling, no question about it. One of the reasons is that education — and American education in particular, because of the standardization...it does not emphasize diversity or individuality; it's not about awakening the student, it's about compliance; and it has a very linear view of life, which is simply not the case with life at all."*
> *-Sir Ken Robinson*

Our world demands something greater and far more complex. At *its* heart it must address sustainability, environmental and planetary of course, but also, inherently *its own*. This will require innovation which itself will require creativity, and whole, imaginative, service-oriented people.

Maria Montessori advocated this long ago: *"Education should no longer be mostly imparting knowledge, but must take a new path, seeking the release of human potential."*

Now, more than ever, we need to create new educational models for our times - designed to intuitively and actively attend to the individual and whole child.

When I decided to go out on my own, I searched for alternative educational models, such as homeschooling (which still generally follows a standard 'Pre-K through 12' course curriculum) and was introduced to the idea of *unschooling*. This happened when I discovered the Sudbury Valley School. Thinking that I was working on an innovative model with I-WE, I was shocked to find this amazing school was founded in 1968.

Sudbury school has had an excellent track record of success with the children who attended over the years. These children got to explore the world at their own pace, in their own unique ways with complete freedom of choice for their activities, and in such a beautiful setting. **Sudbury** is an *unschooling* boarding school, which in my opinion, is a spectacular enterprise. You can find out more about this phenomenal school by visiting their website:

http://www.sudval.org/01_abou_01.html

While writing this book, I came upon another wonderful school that uses so many of our principles, named **Running River**. This school is located in Boulder, Colorado and on their website they have the same video we have on ours from **Sir Kenneth Robinson** about *Changing Paradigms about the Public Education Systems.*

http://runningriver.org/

There is one more school I have found named, **Star School** located in Flagstaff Arizona, serving children K-8 as does **Running River** above**.** I have had the pleasure to visit this school and was so impressed and inspired by all that they have achieved, working with the government as a charter school.

www.starschool.org

There are many hidden treasure schools that I have not yet had the pleasure to find, but just knowing that they are around makes my heart smile. As I discover them, I will continue sharing them.

For now I will leave you with this extra-ordinary open source education platform that is getting richer daily and for whom IWE has been and continues to be a consultant: **One community: Open source education for life.**

One Community is a 501c3 non-profit global transformation organization. The Open Source Education for Life program is the educational component of what they are creating. This program is defined by being:

47

- Free-shared
- Inspiring and fun
- Inclusive of parents
- Comprehensive and adaptable to any environment
- Provided in a manner that we would want to experience as adults
- Applicable and beneficial to all ages and focused equally on how to teach, and how people learn and achieve, as much as what to learn and achieve

The program is for all ages and all learning levels and meant for implementation in homeschooling, traditional schooling, private schooling environments, or included as part of their self-replicating teacher/demonstration communities, villages, and cities model. The program is a constant cooperative evolution including specific sections covering:

- Foundations of Outstanding Leaders, Teachers, and Communicators

- Curriculum for Life - Curriculum designed for every age, infants to adults

- Teaching Strategies for Life - Education strategies for all subjects and ages

- Learning Tools and Toys for Life - Engaging games and other learning aids for all ages

- Lesson Plans for Life - Weekly theme-based lesson plans for all subjects & learning levels

- Evaluation and Evolution - Collaborative "Growth Portfolio" creation and maintenance

- The Ultimate Classroom - Open source educational classroom design and layout details

- Licensing - Sharing the details of our process to create a licensed education program

Putting all of these things together, One Community's mission for this program is to maximize real-world options for all participants and prepare ourselves and our children, through education and application, to be leaders and influential contributors to what we believe is the beginning of a new golden age of innovation, collaboration, creativity, and people living and working together for The Highest Good of All.

If you'd like complete details on this program, with access to all its components, visit:

http://www.onecommunityglobal.org/highest-good-education/

Pie

Did you ever wonder why?
Everyone on earth loves pie?

Maybe because
It tastes so sweet

Or it's what we eat
When we all meet,

But I think it's way more than that,
Not because it can make us fat,

Or that we sit around and chat
Eating it from a plate that's flat

No, these are not the reason
We eat it every single season!

It's what it stands for - now there's a clue
It's what inside your heart does brew,

Because something in us rejoices
Like angel's singing voices
When the pie comes out
There is no doubt,

In pie there is Love,
Yes in Pie there is Love

Created from high above
And the god of pie
That great baker in the sky,

Simply wants us to try
Every flavor before we die!

And that is why
Everyone on earth loves pie!

Don Lamb © 2008

Unschooling and Hackschooling

"It is not so very important for a person to learn facts. For that he does not really need a college. He can learn them from books. The value of an education in a liberal arts college is not learning of many facts but the training of the mind to think something that cannot be learned from textbooks."
-**Albert Einstein**

Unschooling is not easily defined, but I hope these few excerpts will paint a good picture for you. Some of these are from leaders in this field:

From Earl Stevens: *"My answer is that we follow our interests - and our interests inevitably lead to science, literature, history, mathematics, music - all the things that have interested people before anybody thought of them as "subjects." A large component of unschooling is grounded in doing real things, not because we hope they will be good for us, but because they are intrinsically fascinating."* **http://www.naturalchild.org/guest/earl_stevens.html**

From the Family Unschooler Network: *"Our primary purpose in unschooling is to keep alive the spark of curiosity and the natural love of learning with which all children are born. We want our children to accept learning as a natural part of living, and an ongoing process that continues throughout life. We want their learning to remain an integrated process in which all subjects are interrelated. We also want to allow them the time to pursue a subject as fully as they want, rather than imposing artificial time constraints on them. We believe these aspects of learning are limited by the traditional implementation of a curriculum, and we choose to homeschool as a way to circumvent those limitations."*
http://www.unschooling.org/

> *"What does education often do? It makes a straight-cut ditch of a free, meandering brook."*
> **-Henry David Thoreau**

From John Holt who is known for coining the word unschooling in the 1970's: *"When pressed, I define unschooling as allowing children as much freedom to learn in the world, as their parents can comfortably bear. The advantage of this method is that it doesn't require you, the parent, to become someone else, i.e. a professional teacher pouring knowledge into child-vessels on a planned basis. Instead you live and learn together, pursuing questions and interests as they arise and using conventional schooling on an "on demand" basis, if at all. This is the way we learn before going to school and the way we learn when we leave school and enter the world of work."*
http://www.holtgws.com/whatisunschoolin.html

> *"What we want is to see the child in pursuit of knowledge, and not knowledge in pursuit of the child."*
> **-George Bernard Shaw**

From Leo Babauta: *"It's an educational philosophy that provides for more freedom than any other learning method, and prepares kids for an uncertain and rapidly changing future better than anything else I know. Unschoolers learn just like you or I learn as adults: based on what interests them, figuring out how to learn it on their own, changing as they change, using whatever resources and learning materials they find, driven by curiosity and practical application rather than because someone says it's important."*
http://zenhabits.net/unschool/

> *"Governments want efficient technicians, not human beings, because human beings become dangerous to governments – and to organized religions as well. That is why governments and religious organizations seek to control education."*
> **-Jiddu Krishnamurti**

The 'most watched' TED talk of all times, was the speech that **Sir Ken Robinson** gave on education, *How Schools Kill Creativity*:

http://www.ted.com/talks/ken_robinson_says_schools_kill_creativity.html

> *"The fact is that given the challenges we face, education doesn't need to be reformed -- it needs to be transformed. The key to this transformation is not to standardize education, but to personalize it, to build achievement on discovering the individual talents of each child, to put students in an environment where they want to learn and where they can naturally discover their true passions."*
> **-Sir Ken Robinson**

Recently, thirteen-year-old Logan LaPlante spoke on TED about Hackshooling. He portrays what I envision is possible for all children if given the opportunity to escape from the public education system:
http://www.youtube.com/watch?v=h11u3vtcpaY

> *"You have a right to experiment with your life. You will make mistakes. And they are right too. No, I think there was too rigid a pattern. You came out of an education and are supposed to know your vocation. Your vocation is fixed, and maybe ten years later you find you are not a teacher anymore or you're not a painter anymore. It may happen. It has happened. I mean Gauguin decided at a certain point he wasn't a banker anymore; he was a painter. And so he walked away from banking. I think we have a right to change course. But society is the one that keeps demanding that we fit in and not disturb things. They would like you to fit in right away so that things work now."*
> **-Anais Nin**

I-WE is aligned with the unschooling philosophy on many levels, even though we provide a more defined structure, especially for the younger children. For those six years old and above, we have leaders from the community who we recommend along with wonderful programs, such as those Logan described in his TED talk. We believe clearer guidelines than those provided in the unschooling journey are often needed to support families who choose an alternative model of education for their children. This is especially relevant for working families and crucial for underprivileged children. The truth is not many feel totally capable of taking their children's education into their own hands.

> *"Education is what remains after one has forgotten everything he learned in school." ... "The only thing that interferes with my learning is my education."*
> **-Albert Einstein**

The information that follows is provided especially for those interested in starting an I-WE program in their community. In the next chapters, we will outline the pillars of the I-WE philosophy, the core activities of this education opportunity, and give you an idea of what an I-WE home-classroom would look like, as well as an outdoor play area. We will discuss some of the unique traits, such as the mixed age groups idea, which expands beyond Maria Montessori's three-year span. We gather with youth ages 2-27, for activities such as welcoming morning circles, meal preparations and cleanups, or the building of a treehouse, where everyone can have a part in the fulfillment of the project.

> *"Common sense is in spite of, not the result of, education."*
> **-Victor Hugo**

The Measure of Success

In this article published online March 27th, 2012 by **Cassi** 4 In *Musings, Unschooling theories*, **Cassi** addresses the questions posed about the success rate of unschooling. I have taken bits of her answers so you can get a general idea, but you can go to her website to read more of her great posts:

http://www.unschoolingblog.com

How many of them go to college? What kinds of jobs do they get?

"*Daniel Greenberg of Sudbury Valley School has said on more than one occasion that 100% of SVS students who want to go to college get in, and usually to their first choice. …There was also an off-handed statement about the fact that 80% of SVS students do go to college…*"

Those of us in the unschooling/free schooling community do not see college attendance or career choice and subsequent salary as a Measure of Success. A.S. Neill was known to say, and I think I've quoted it here before, that he would rather Summerhill produce a happy street sweeper than a neurotic prime minister. So, the Measure of Success, from my view would be how happy and fulfilled the graduate is in his or her life…. Can you measure happiness?" **Cassi.**

> "It is not education, but education of a certain kind, that will serve us. And the current model of Western, urban-centered, school-based education, which is so often more focused on turning children into efficient corporate units rather than curious and open-minded adults, will only lead us further down the wrong path."
> -**David W. Orr**

This Quote was taken from a website dedicated to research on the Gross National Happiness, a term coined by the Fourth King of Bhutan in the 1970's, along with this information:

The four pillars of this measurement are:

- Good governance

- Sustainable socio-economic development

- Cultural preservation

- Environmental conservation

These four pillars were further classified in 9 domains:

- Psychological well-being

- Standard of living and happiness

- Good governance and gross national happiness

- Health

- Education

- Community vitality

- Cultural diversity and resilience

- Time use and happiness

- Ecological diversity and resilience.

You can find more about this on the website:

http://www.grossnationalhappiness.com/

End of a circle song with our wonderful Play-based & Waldorf trained teacher, Miss Andrea

Learning to navigate in the city…

And in the wild!

**I-WE end of summer
camping trip
in the redwoods**

THE VISION OF I-WE

> *"Nobody else can make anybody else learn anything anymore than if you are a gardener, you can make flowers grow. You don't sit there and stick the petals on and put the leaves on and paint it. The flower grows itself. Your job, if you are any good at it, is to provide the optimum conditions for it to do that, to allow it to grow itself."*
> **-Sir Ken Robinson**

IMAGINE WISDOM EDUCATION, known as I-WE, recognizes every child as a wise and divine being. We empower students ages 2-27, to discover and share their unique gifts, in service to the community (come-unity), as soon as they desire.

> *"A healthy social life is found only when in the mirror of each soul, the whole community finds its reflection, and when in the whole community, the virtue of each one is living."*
> **-Rudolf Steiner** *(Waldorf)*

Embracing Love as foundation and Imagination as inspiration, I-WE utilizes Howard Gardner's strategies of multiple intelligences and honors ancient native teachings through storytelling and circles, as well as meditation/yoga practices. I-WE expands essential concepts from early educational models such as Montessori and Waldorf, and moves toward unschooling for children six and older.

> *"The Internet is becoming the town square for the global village of tomorrow."*
> **-Bill Gates**

I-WE prepares its students for global living and peaceful leadership that honors all beings with a sustainable living focus. Entrepreneurial skills are acquired at an early age through apprenticeships with passionate leaders from the community. Celebration of diversity and culture is reinforced with foreign languages, compassionate communication, community service and a web connection with others around the world.

> *"In the U.K, I have been lobbying the government to do entrepreneurial loans instead of student loans… For some people it's much better to just get out in the real word and say, "Screw it, let's do it" and give it a go. You learn so much from being in the jungle and building a business from scratch."*
> -**Sir Richard Branson** – Virgin Galactic

I-WE is an unschooling model with a twist. The biggest twist is that for the first four years of the child's education period (2-6 years of age), we offer a great variety of stimulating activities for the child in a very structured and prepared environment.

> *"The early years, from about 2-1/2 to 6 years of age, are critical for children as they develop many of their attitudes, interests, basic skills, and approaches to life, family, and society — the aspects of living that are so important to becoming a well-rounded, confident, stable person who can contribute to the happiness and prosperity of others who interact with him or her all the way into the future."*
> -**The Whole Child Montessori**
> http://www.wholechildmontessori.org/montessori/

The I-WE education honors the child's spirit first and foremost, in all aspects of it's blossoming. An I-WE teacher seeks to understand the individual needs of each child and to create individual curriculums; shifting 'development' from a theory on paper, to an active, intuitive framework for personal development. Once the child reaches the age of six and has received the structured foundation within the rich and prepared environment, the model becomes somewhat of an unschooling approach. The child chooses which subjects he/she wants to explore based on his/her interests, desires, curiosities and passions. As parents and teachers, we continue to introduce community leaders to the child and bring the child to the world, locally and globally.

Following is a beautiful representation of one of the results I-WE is striving to achieve with its students:

An anthropologist proposed a game to the kids in an African tribe:

He put a basket full of fruit near a tree and told the kids that whoever got there first would win the sweet fruits. When he told them to run they all took each other's hands and ran together, then sat together enjoying their treats. When he asked them why they had run like that as one could have had all the fruits for him/herself, they said:

"UBUNTU, how can one of us be happy

if all the other ones are sad?"

'UBUNTU' in the Xhosa culture means:

"I am because we are."

ABOUT LEADERSHIP:

*"Having a personality
of caring about people is
important.*

*You can't be a good leader
unless you generally like people.
That is how you bring out
the best in them...*

ABOUT EDUCATION:

*Education doesn't just take place in
stuffy classrooms and university
buildings, it can happen
everywhere,
every day,
to every person."*

-Sir Richard Branson

WHO CAN START AN I-WE SCHOOL?

Anyone can! YOU can!

"Education breeds confidence. Confidence breeds hope. Hope breeds peace… It does not matter how slowly you go as long as you do not stop."
-**Confucius**

**It doesn't take a lot of room,
as children are little**

**What seems small to us,
is quite large to them**

> *"You don't learn to walk by following rules. You learn by doing, and by falling over."... "I was dyslexic, I had no understanding of schoolwork whatsoever. I certainly would have failed IQ tests. And it was one of the reasons I left school when I was 15 years old. And if I - if I'm not interested in something, I don't grasp it."... "Although my spelling is still sometimes poor, I have managed to overcome the worst of my difficulties through training myself to concentrate."*
> **-Sir Richard Branson**

If your child is one of the 2 out of 7 children who *do* thrive in the public school system, then the I-WE Model can be used to enrich his or her educational experience, as a complement to feed his or her soul.

> *"We have to go from what is essentially an industrial model of education, a manufacturing model, which is based on linearity and conformity and batching people. We have to move to a model that is based more on principles of agriculture. We have to recognize that human flourishing is not a mechanical process; it's an organic process. And you cannot predict the outcome of human development. All you can do, like a farmer, is create the conditions under which they will begin to flourish."*
> **-Sir Ken Robinson**

But if you, like us, believe that the public education system is outdated or has broken too many young souls, and you want to do something about it, use this model to start your own private school.

> According to one of our advisory members, KT, who has successfully unschooled both of her daughters during middle school and high school, her girls are both now very successful in their fields. One of her daughter, who just turned thirty, is the executive director of an East Coast community-television station. She never graduated high school; her experience, self-confidence and intuitive wisdom are her tools. Her other daughter is thirty-three-year old and is an informational architect in the AP field. She graduated with honors in her field of computer science.

How to Legally Unschool Your Children

"Records are made to be broken. It is in man's nature to continue to strive to do just that."
-**Sir Richard Branson**

We will show you how you can legally do this, easily, in most every state in the U.S and with a bit more effort in a few others. Most daycare facilities will be allowed to have the mixed aged group of children in their homes (unlike in a preschool setting where children under five must be separate then their older siblings. But it is important that you check with your local authorities to see what the law will or will not permit.

"Homeschooling is the recognized name as far as the government goes. To comply with California's governmental requirements, I found through my research, forming a private school is the best bet.

Once that is accomplished, you can form your own educational system. Unschooling is the specific name for empowering your children and yourself to follow and support the intuition and passion of your children while giving them the balance of safe boundaries as they navigate planet Earth.

A necessary requirement of unschooling is to want to be the one who teaches and learns from the children, to be with them rather than turning them over to someone who does not have the same value system, to be the child's protector and the one who guides them in a loving and responsible manner, teaching by example. In other words, children need clear boundaries to learn about navigating safely, and becoming aware of consequences that come with their actions, based on common sense and consciousness.

As parents do the research necessary to form a private school in their particular neighborhood, they will learn what is required by the state, so their child's education can take place in a safe learning environment. From my own experience, I have found that once the form is set in place, the parents will have free rein (within the requirements) to run their school as they wish." K.T.

This is a link explaining what you must do to legally stop going to school. Option #1 is recommended by a group in Los Angeles who we were heart-storming with a couple of years ago.

http://www.californiahomeschool.net/howTo/legOpt.htm

Here are a couple of links to support you in this process from Sandra Dodd, who is one of the pioneers in supporting families in this path:

http://sandradodd.com/unschooling

http://sandradodd.com/portfolio

http://sandradodd.com/unschoolingcurriculum.html

Even an alley will work, when you find your loving and creative community!

THE MISSION OF I-WE

"There is no school equal to a decent home and no teacher equal to a virtuous parent."
-**Mahatma Gandhi**

At I-WE, we understand a child's strongest role model is his or her parents, teachers, and other members of his or her support team at school. If we can all embody the spirit of love in our lives, the deep experience of love will become a natural way of life. The child will feel safe to express his or herself and trust any outcome. For it is through this great feeling of love and joy, that we will all experience peace and unlimited abundance in body, mind and spirit.

"The giving of Love is an education in itself."
-**Eleanor Roosevelt**

The I-WE model serves young people ages 2-27, in a very interactive, community based curriculum. With a strong multisensory foundation, our program has the flexibility and resilience to address each child's needs as they arise. Our youth are encouraged to mentor younger children, serving as strong role models for them during the learning process. This enables the older children to develop leadership skills, while providing the younger ones support from their 'school heroes and heroines'.

The mission of IMAGINE WISDOM EDUCATION (I-WE) is to offer a loving and enriching education that empowers children to realize their greatest potential. Learners ask: "Who am I? What are my gifts? How can I contribute?" This discovery of the Self serves as a transforming catalyst, turning play into the pursuit of wholeness and peaceful leadership. It has been said: "Children learn best when they are known, explore their passions and engage all of their senses."

"Our care of the child should be governed, not by the desire to make him learn things, but by the endeavor always to keep burning within him that light which is called intelligence."
-**Maria Montessori**

I-WE encourages students to develop and achieve at their own pace, as well as supporting them to share their gifts and realize their dreams. This process is based upon Maslow's hierarchy of growth and development. The curriculum is emergent, as well as guided, and provides the structure for discovery, safety and freedom to imagine. The environment is co-created to inspire, motivate and teach, as well as reflect the children's individual and collective visions.

> *"I am convinced that love is the most durable power in the world. It is not an expression of impractical idealism, but of practical realism. Far from being the pious injunction of a Utopian dreamer, love is an absolute necessity for the survival of our civilization..."*
> **-Martin Luther King, Jr.**

I-WE embraces love as the core value of its program and utilizes Howard Gardner's strategies of multiple intelligences (Linguistic, Logical-Mathematical, Spatial, Musical, Bodily-Kinesthetic, Interpersonal, Intrapersonal and Naturalistic - and informally two more: existential and pedagogical). Our curriculum is dynamic and integrative. We are committed to helping children develop to their highest potential, spiritually, mentally, emotionally and physically, with a strong emphasis upon the use of imagination throughout their entire education.

> *"Imagination is the source of every form of human achievement. And it's the one thing that I believe we are systematically jeopardizing in the way we educate our children and ourselves."*
> **-Sir Ken Robinson**

I-WE communities include daily circle time with the use of a talking stick to facilitate group discussions. The talking stick is also used in times of conflict, when two or more individuals are in need of an intentional dialogue.

> *"Peace does not mean an absence of conflicts; differences will always be there. Peace means solving these differences through peaceful means; through dialogue, education, knowledge; and through humane ways."*
> **-Dalai Lama XIV**

Conscious and compassionate communication is practiced daily. We combine teachings from Marshall Rosenberg's *Non-Violent Communication (NVC)*, and *Imago Dialogue*, memorialized by Harville Hendrix in his book titled: *Getting the Love You Want*. NVC offers tools to reduce violence and create peace, by identifying and sharing feelings and needs. Imago consists of *Mirroring* the message received, *Validating* the person for feeling the way they feel (even if not agreeing with their view), *Empathizing* and lastly, *Making a Request*, which turns a frustration into a *Gift* to be received. Both are extremely powerful methods for mastering compassionate and empathic communication.

> *"Don't believe what your eyes are telling you. All they show is limitation. Look with your understanding, find out what you already know, and you'll see the way to fly."*
> **-Richard Bach**

Many of us also realize that our world has become a great deal more complex since the educational models we have inherited were developed. As a result of this, the children and their families are encouraged to participate in personal development and outdoor educational programs to help them grow strong and resilient for the exciting new world that is emerging.

Here are some of the courses we recommend:

The Landmark Forum is an educational program for children ages eight and up, as well as for teenager and adults.

http://www.landmarkworldwide.com/

The Ropes Course Challenge provides an outdoor personal development and team-building program.

http://fulcrumadventures.com/ropes-course-challenge.html

Earthroots is another local to Laguna Beach, outdoor program that helps deepen children's connection with nature. Look for others like it in your area:

http://earthrootsfieldschool.org/

Following, are a couple organizations worth learning about:

A wonderful non-denominational International Spiritual Center called **AGAPE** has inspiring weekly complementary programs every Wednesday evening & Sunday mornings for all ages, from infants to teens held during the regular services. There are also retreats for all ages during the annual Revelation Conference * and then terrific summer camps with The Agape Youth Community ** and an amazing summer school program that includes music, nature, field trips, arts & crafts, as well as The Agape CDF Freedom Schools program. For more details, please see:
http://agapelive.com/

A beautiful, loving, giving, humanitarian and special woman that is considered a living Saint named **AMMACHI** * (also warmly regarded as **Amma** ~ The Hugging saint) has a U.S. summer tour every Year. She visits major cities across the US spreading unconditional love, giving hugs, and uniting communities & families with a shared purpose of helping others. And there are excellent children's programs, family retreats and incredible opportunities for the little ones to play, learn, grow, sing, dance, meditate, do yoga and be in joy while supporting charities. To learn more, visit:
http://amma.org/

Lastly, I-WE recommends the children build their own school, classroom or outdoor play space, such as adding tree houses and other creative projects, using their vision and imagination. If possible, at the initial gathering, have the children participate in adding artistic value to their play space and "work" space. The time spent co-creating this way will bring great joy and value to the children.

These long-term group projects offer in-depth experiential learning and, when completed, a great sense of accomplishment for all involved. In addition, it provides the children with opportunities to learn cooperation, creativity, communication skills and problem solving. Through their physical labor, the deep beauty they created together will continue to live within their hearts, as a visceral experience, a treasure that will last for the rest of their lives.

Some examples might include the children cutting boards or hammering nails for the tree house, making the cement and putting it in the ground, or painting tiles to go into one of the murals. Children of all ages can participate in this effort, making it a fantastic opportunity to connect the young ones and older members of the I-WE community. Together they could do what they can never do alone and this synergy expands their confidence to manifest their dreams.

Damien, our Teepee builder from the Navaho Reservation and the Math teacher of Rock Point Community School, is waiting for us to call him for his help!

Both Pink Lily Flowers, SAME BUT DIFFERENT!

"You are one of a kind and unique. Never forget that."
-Richard Simmons

THE 6 PILLARS OF I-WE'S STARGAZER LILIES

There are six pillars representing our educational philosophy. A pillar is often defined as being a firm, insulated support for a structure. The pillars are the principles necessary to uphold the I-WE standard of excellence we strive to achieve. Each one serves as a vital component to the model. However, it is not until they are joined together in harmony, that their synergy can create the power and stability needed for the I-WE model to flourish as a Global Educational Community.

The essential aspects of the 6 pillars can be compared to the six parts of my favorite flowers, the Stargazer **L.I.L.I.E.S.** The petals/sepals are delicate in form, yet they also are also strong and resilient. And their scent is divine! Much like the grace and beauty contained within the Lilies, we feel the six pillars of the I-WE program contain fundamental principles needed to heal our planet.

Lakota Instructions for Living

*"Friend do it this way - that is,
Whatever you do in life,
Do the very best you can
With both your heart and mind.*

*And if you do it that way,
The Power of the Universe
Will come to your assistance,
If your heart and mind are in Unity.*

*When one sits in the Hoop of the People,
One must be responsible because
All of Creation is related.
And the hurt of one is the hurt of all.
And the honor of one is the honor of all.*

*And whatever we do affects
Everything in the universe.
If you do it that way - that is,
If you truly join your heart and mind
As One - whatever you ask for,
That's the Way It's Going To Be."*
-Buffalo Calf Woman

1. Love – A 'Win-Win' Experience for Everyone

Everything we do in our life can be a genuine win-win for everyone; Love is a key ingredient in our everyday activities. Love is our most important practice and the essential foundation of all we do. Love permeates all aspects of our lives, whether it is at school, at home, or out in the world. It affects our choices for education, relationships, diet and nutrition, career, and finances. As a result, the more we love ourselves, our children and one another, the more conscious and loving choices we can make in each moment of our lives.

> *"Our task must be to free ourselves by widening our circle of compassion to embrace all living creatures and the whole of nature and its beauty."*
> **-Albert Einstein**

Here is a thought-provoking quote representing 'win-win' in relation to our food choices:

> *"Some of the best things about being a vegetarian include, of course:*
> *- Contributing towards the welfare of animals.*
> *- Being a vegetarian can also make you a healthier person.*
> *- It helps the environment!*
> *All of these things make vegetarianism worthwhile.*
> *It's really a win-win situation."*
> **-Laura Manneli**

Another way that love and win-win are expressed, in the I-WE model, is through cooperation and co-creation for the highest good of all instead of competition and scarcity consciousness. We strive to improve ourselves based upon our past performances, rather than comparing ourselves to other people. We play, and live fully, so that everybody wins, not just a few. We give thanks for the strengths of others and give back with our own individual talents.

"Imagine all the people

Living life in peace

You may say I'm a dreamer

But I'm not the only one

I hope someday you'll join us

And the world will be as one."

-John Lennon

2. Imagine... Full Self-Expression

"Imagination is more important than knowledge."
-**Albert Einstein**

Imagination is the second fundamental element that we nurture in an I-WE environment. We use all forms of creative arts. We learn about ourselves through play, drama, storytelling, group projects, alone 'work' time, and natural problem solving. Many of our activities serve to support and guide the discovery of individual gifts and passions.

"Everyone has a gift not only vital to themselves, as an individual but to their community."
-**Sobonfu Somé**

We believe that every child is born with unique and special gifts that, if cultivated, will serve the highest good of all. Freedom of choice is key. We encourage free self-expression in all ways that are safe and honor the community (always considerate of causing no harm).

Co-creating with the Fairies...

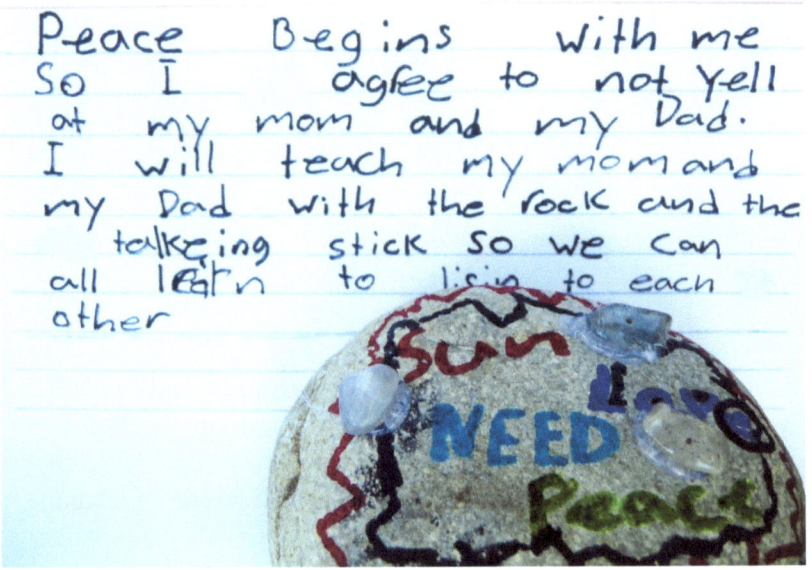

**This was written
by a
7 year-old-boy
in a
Genius Connections
Playshop!**

3. Leaders in Peace, Health and Happiness

> *"The first wealth is health."*
> -Ralph Waldo Emerson

Our definition of leadership embraces the new paradigm of serving others in a collaborative way that empowers the individuals as well as the community. How is this leadership contributing towards the health, happiness and prosperity of each person in the community? Leaders are made, not born, as some believe. Yes, there are those for whom it is more natural to lead, but the qualities that make a great leader can be developed and nurtured.

> *"Intelligence plus character - that is the goal of true education."*
> -Martin Luther King Jr.

I-WE offers such development and nurturing for our young adults, ages thirteen to twenty-seven, through our *Progressive Team* program. This program connects the youth with local businesses to provide a mutually beneficial opportunity; the business benefits by having some additional help, and the youth benefit by gaining some 'real-world' experience and a little pocket money. This arrangement is more of a paid internship, rather than a part-time job. This is frequently the place where relationships are fostered and apprenticeships evolve over time.

We need leaders at this time who are genuine and care for the highest good of all beings. We encourage young people to develop strong values as they grow into their leadership roles.

This is a list of recognized leadership qualities that can be acquired by experience and developed, which we strive to cultivate in I-WE communities:

- Honesty
- Trust
- Being Coachable
- Intuition
- Teamwork
- Confidence
- Positive Attitude
- Effective Communication
- Creativity
- Sense of Humor
- Ability to Inspire

I-WE's curriculum is designed to nurture and evolve strong, resilient, and peaceful leaders who can provide a powerful and heartfelt contribution to the 21st century.

> *"Our greatest happiness does not depend on the condition of life in which chance has placed us, but is always the result of a good conscience, good health, occupation, and freedom in all just pursuits."*
> -**Thomas Jefferson**

Many believe as we do, that life is lived *Inside-Out*. We nourish the spirit of each child by helping them develop peace and happiness within themselves. This positive feeling will then be reflected back into the world. We celebrate diversity and joyfully include those less privileged children in our programs as a form of service and contribution to the community at large.

> *"A hero is an ordinary individual who finds the strength to persevere and endure in spite of overwhelming obstacles."*
> -**Christopher Reeve**

We teach foreign languages to help broaden the children's awareness of other cultures and empower them to experience a global perspective in their education. Additionally adding one or more foreign language early on, has tremendous value. It not only is beneficial to the intellect of the child, but also fosters the imagination and helps with abstract thinking. Bi-lingual children have greater problem solving abilities from which our world can greatly benefit. The children are also introduced to many great leaders and teachers throughout history, as well as a wide variety of contemporary heroes. These people serve as strong role models to inspire the youth as they grow and develop in their maturity.

"Personal transformation can and does have global effects. As we go, so goes the world, For the world is us. The revolution that will save the world is ultimately a personal one."

-Marianne Williamson

Practicing leadership

4. Indigenous Roots & Evolutionary Consciousness

*"Treat the earth well.
It was not given to you by your parents.
It was loaned to you by your children.
We do not inherit the Earth from our Ancestors,
We borrow it from our Children."*
-Ancient Native American Proverb

We honor many schools of ancient wisdom and are committed to forging a movement for the conscious evolution of our planet, with great reverence for both the indigenous ways and the evolutionary consciousness yearning to be realized. We often sit on the ground while we 'work' close to the earth, using our voices and drums to communicate in sacred ways. This helps ground everyone and deepens our rhythmic connection to the universal flow of life energy.

"Humankind has not woven the web of life. We are but one thread within it. Whatever we do to the web, we do to ourselves. All things are bound together. All things connect."
-Chief Seattle, 1854

Storytelling is a big part of the way we share wisdom with the children. Often we ask our community elders to come and share stories with our youth. We have a Native American Elder, Orville Mestes, who is in the process of recording some of the traditional oral stories from his Lakota lineage, which we hope to have available in the near future. We utilize puppets, and write our own stories, poetry and songs. We especially integrate storytelling to keep our young children's yoga practices fun and interesting. We call those stories "Yogi Tales." and all children are encouraged to co-create additional fun stories with their yoga teammates.

"Storytelling is an important part of human continuity."
-Robert Redford

We vision together about the future we wish to manifest. This is done through the use of collages, guided meditations, and setting far-reaching, yet, measurable goals. *As* **Norman Vincent Peale** *states: "Imagination is the true magic carpet."* We dream beyond the knowing of how the future will be realized and call forth all aspects of modern magic on that journey...

5. *Empathic Listening & Compassionate Communication*

"Love and compassion are necessities, not luxuries. Without them humanity cannot survive."
-**Dalai Lama**

Empathic Listening and Compassionate Communication is a daily practice we actively pursue throughout all of our activities. We use a focused daily practice of twenty minutes of mirroring and communication to help us deepen our ability to connect with one another. Our intention is to model loving kindness and mindfulness practices. We encourage everyone to learn through living in the moment with deep listening to our own needs while respecting the needs of others. And we remind each other that we have two ears and only one mouth, so that we might practice listening more deeply to one another and speaking from the heart.

"I like to listen. I have learned a great deal from listening carefully. Most people never listen."
-**Ernest Hemingway**

**These wonderful
litte girls heard,
through story telling,
about
the lack of water
in African villages
and
are imitating
the mamas
who carry
their babies
on their back
and
walk miles
for clean water!**

6. Sustainable Living, Service and Self-Realization through YOGA

> *"We have a moral responsibility to protect the earth and ensure that our children and grandchildren have a healthy and sustainable environment in which to live."*
> **-Jim Clyburn**

Sustainable Living is taught with a deep reverence for our Mother Earth, an understanding of the cycle of life through growing our own food, recycling our leftovers, and collecting our rainwater. We have discussions about global warming, GMOs (Genetically Modified Organisms), and how to preserve our natural resources. Our connection to Mother Earth is deep and is truly our conduit to our spiritual source individually, and as a global community, on this planet and beyond.

> *"Innovations that are guided by smallholder farmers, adapted to local circumstances, and sustainable for the economy and environment will be necessary to ensure food security in the future."*
> **-Bill Gates**

Service is another important part of our curriculum. We give the children many opportunities to serve their local neighborhood, as well as their community at large. This year, in 2014, at our yearly Green Valentines Festival, the children cooked a meal to raise funds to build a well in Africa. Susan Hough, one of our wonderful teachers has been 'Walking for Water' with teenagers for over ten years and has helped build over thirty wells thus far.

> *"The best way to find yourself is to lose yourself in the service of others... Yet Service, which is rendered without joy, helps neither the servant nor the served. But all other pleasures and possessions pale into nothingness before service, which is rendered in a spirit of joy."*
> **-Mahatma Gandhi**

Self-realization through Yoga is designed to encourage each student to 'Know Thyself' by implementing physical asanas (yogic postures), short silent meditation periods, and conscious breathing techniques, into the daily curriculum. Yoga games are included to help the children increase their inner listening skills and to deepen their intuition.

> *"If every 8 year old in the world is taught meditation, we will eliminate violence from the world within one generation."*
> **-Dalai Lama**

A deep sense of peace and wellbeing is assured, when reverence and gratitude become part of us. Through practices such as conscious breathing and mindful eating, we are reminded we are all part of the great "circle of life." This helps us feel more love and compassion for ourselves, and a deeper sense of connection with all beings, everywhere.

> *"...Mother Earth: We have gathered for the healing of all of your children, The Stone People, the Plant People, The four-legged, the two-legged, the creepy crawlers, the Finned, the Furred, and the Winged Ones, All our Relations...."*
> **-The Four Winds Society Prayer**

I-WE children love YOGA

Older children helping younger ones is such a "Win-Win" experience

SUSTAINABLE LIVING

GREEN VALENTINES

Above is our program for the 2014 festival. Only those under twenty-seven years old were invited to take the microphone to educate us, or share what was on their minds about Sustainable Living, so that we, as community, could better support them into creating a brighter future for themselves ☺.

February 8, 2014:

5th Annual Green Valentines Festival. Hundreds of people have come together for this FREE community event of fun, great music, children's activities, and local vendors.

Green Valentines originated out of my desire to give back to our community for the extraordinary support our family received when our beautiful son Christofer was diagnosed with an inoperable brain tumor. During the last 8 months of Christofer's life, praying for a miracle and doing everything we could to save him, our community came together, offering loving support. This emotional, spiritual, and financial generosity was life saving for us. Words cannot express the depth of my gratitude. Christofer's life and our loss taught us how incredible it is when people come together in love.

Because of my stand for the children, I have to say that the 2014 festival was the one that brings the most joy to my heart. It was all about the children and their future. I actually hope that hearts will be so ignited that projects will be birthed from this gathering, as many others have because of our Angel Christofer.

Throughout the years I have heard so many times people saying things like: *"We met at your festival and now we are… going into prisons and making a difference."* – **Susan Hough and Shakti Tribe**; or *"I bought a guitar at your fundraiser and music started flowing through me and I wrote my first album."* – **Chris Amodeo**; or *"I designed an Eco Baby Furniture line because of Christofer."* -**Debi Bodinus.**. Others, simply, but nonetheless very deep: *"My heart opened because of him… I am reminded every day of the blessings my children are, even when I am tired or they are acting out."*

The feedback I receive and comments I hear are endless and inspiring. I am so grateful, and that is why I continue to spend hours in preparation *to bring Community together and to help heal our Earth Mother*.

This first edition of the I-WE educational model was being birthed at that time, so that copies could be available at the festival. Truth is that, two months before, my son Christofer, with whom I still communicate telepathically from the other side of the veil, asked me to stop all my other activities and write the book. Because I always listen to him, I began, not really knowing why he was asking as he just said: "For the next three weeks, you need to work on the I-WE book." This book is a result of this work and of all the synchronistic magic surrounding this first inspiration.

Christofer was kind in giving me the time I needed to deliver this with ease and grace but… Because I didn't work on it as much as I needed to during those initial three weeks, I spent the last three weeks before the festival rushing to get it completed in time. I am amazed by all the Living Angels from the community who came to my rescue, to make sure that this book would be done in time for the special event. These wonderful people are acknowledged at the end of the book, but I am so grateful that they are worth acknowledging twice. I truly do not know how I ever lived without community before and, can no longer even imagine living any other way.

I believe that the world must be longing for this, and it is time. That is what I am feeling deep within my soul, and through my connection with my son and Angel Christofer.

A Valentine for Mother Earth

THE CLASSROOM
YOUR PREPARED ENVIRONMENT

"The environment itself will teach the child, if every error he makes is manifest to him, without the intervention of a parent or teacher, whom should remain a quiet observer of all that happens."
-Maria Montessori

**Give it an air of magic and enchantment
Inviting the children to enter…**

Add color, textures and light!

**When the shelves are covered,
it is easy to make a circle and no one is distracted**

It is also easy to dance, play, or do yoga

**This is also the way we prepare for our nap time
with mats and blankets**

**We play meditation music and
use aromatherapy
to help soothe
the children
into deep and peaceful rest** ☺

When it is time to "work," as children do for a brief period daily in an I-WE classroom, the curtains are opened and the "work" period begins. These can last anywhere from twenty to forty minutes, depending upon how focused the group is. If need be, it can be broken down into two separate work periods with a dance, drum or an outdoor break. Children work on mats on the floor, one activity at a time and usually by themselves. There are some exceptions where two or more children can participate in a focused "work" activity, but this doesn't happen in the beginning of a school year.

The main objective is to teach the children to follow their heart and make choices. We ask them to work quietly so that other children can "work" peacefully as well. We use the "work" time period to allow each child to choose activities that feed their desire in the moment.

These would all be considered "work" stations

Taking a sensorial, spatial and visual experience…

to pen and paper… Well done!

The children practice playing/working by themselves along with taking and putting work back on the shelf, one at a time. This helps the children have order outside, which reflects inside their brain, thus helping them feel calm and organized.

The moveable wooden alphabet is an extra-ordinary tool designed by Maria Montessori. This wooden set of alphabet letters provides such ease for small children, whose fingers are not yet strong enough to write nice letters on paper, to be able to make words and practice their language skills, using many of their sences.

Team work

Older child teaching math to toddlers

**Snack time looking
at the garden and butterflies…**

And then… There is Music and Dance…

Our teens love to play music together too!

Water blessing at San Onofre

Led by Dr. Emoto and,

Hopi peace ambassador, Ruben Saufkie

Satyanna at a sunset yoga class

during a Genius Connection Playshop

PLAY AREA

Make it fun so the children can

Crawl around

Build things

Actively play

Run and

Explore!

Young children love these outdoor tents

And soft cozy places to rest or read

If at all possible, use a natural area, or create a structure for the children to safely climb or to test their balancing skills

Such pleasure playing with mud…

To run and chase each other…

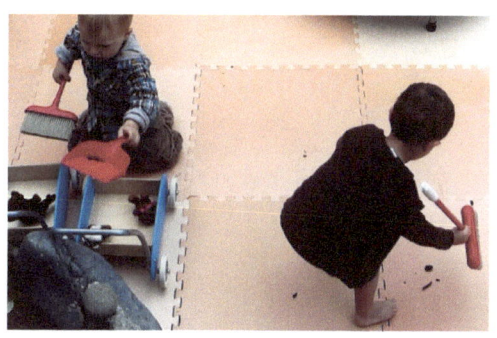

Preparing for life

**… or mindfully…
help an ant out of the way, to safety!**

**'Mommy and me' program
for our youngest members**

Mixed Ages in Harmony and Thriving

Learning about Crystals with Debi McKee

Fashion Design Week with Debi

OUR LAGUNA BEACH TEAM
DURING THE FIRST FIVE YEARS OF DEVELOPMENT

VISIONARY/FOUNDER

SATYANNA CHRIS LUKEN

Satyanna@me.com 949-412-8948

Montessori, French and Yoga Teacher

Photographer

Author of "ABC of Conscious Parenting
- Agreements Before (and after) Conceiving
And I-WE Imagine Wisdom Education ☺

Green Valentines Festival Organizer

Public Speaker

Health Promoter

Children Advocate

OUR COMMUNITY LEADERS AND I-WE TEACHERS

This was our team in Laguna Beach, CA...

Your team can be made of similar community leaders, or it could be completely different, depending upon your environment and which part of the world is your home. That is not important. What is important is that you handpick the people you admire most from your community and ask them to participate in the education of your children! You will be amazed at the response most great leaders have to this opportunity, especially from the elders.

CATHERINE AMANDA CLARK, Ed. D. - Our Selfhood Master Teacher

Catherine has taught part-time in Africa for 20 years and is a doll maker who creates images that address social injustice. She has a non-profit organization, which makes dolls for helping children of trauma. Her extensive background in the arts and child development and her interest in nurturing wholeness, are reflected in her two books on the subject of development of selfhood. A graduate of Pacific Oaks College, Catherine has an Early Childhood Credential, Masters Degree in Human Development and African Studies and a Doctorate in Education from Fielding Graduate University. She has committed to working 10-20 hours per week with the I-WE children.

STEVE BLAZER - Retired Master Waldorf Teacher - Committed to 10 hours a week with the children, doing Seasonal and Rhythmic activities with the children.

CARON COLE - "I have almost 30 years experience as a Special Educator, serving all age levels and levels of disabilities. I currently serve as Education Specialist at the district level.

I oversee 12 schools, middle, high and adult transition programs, as well as the New Teachers Trainings (I have 13 this year!) and I teach the Non-violent Crisis Intervention and Prevention Program as I have my 8 to Great Certification." She is eager to join I-WE full time.

LINDA CROW - Native American Teachings

Native American Drumming, Singing and Dancing for Children of all Ages and Challenges. "My Cheyenne Mom's last wish was for me to teach these ways to the Children, for they are our Future. And then these Sacred Traditions cannot be lost." AH-HO! Linda Crow is eager to share these songs and dances with the I-WE students.

NANCY DANTONI - Special Facilitator of our Youth Ages 16-27 is committed to empowering this group of our youth that is often thought of as ready for independent living, yet still can use loving guidance, listening and recognition.

ANA GONZALEZ - Our Master Spanish Teacher has a BA in Psychology and over 10 years of teaching experience with children of all ages. She taught in the nursery, preschool & Kindergarten, and also substituted for grade school ages at Anneliese Academy. She is one of eight children and mother of two bilingual children herself. Has committed to 10-20 hours with the I-WE students.

Ana and Magela Teaching Spanish ☺

SUSAN HOUGH - Our Master Ritual and Ancient Wisdom Teacher with Sobonfu will be assisting I-WE students with Rites of Passage, which are so important. We are so blessed to bring these rituals back to our community. Susan has a Bachelor's of Social Work and over 30 years of experience working in mental health facilities and adolescent treatment programs.

In addition, Susan has completed healing and ritual trainings with Mary Branch Grove, Mietek Wirkus, and Sobonfu Somé. She is also nationally recognized for her work with Somé's non-profit Wisdom Springs as the Director for its annual teen fundraising project, *Walking for Water,* that has raised over $250,000 for the construction of wells in developing countries, including Burkina Faso.

Susan helps the teens 'find their gift' within the many aspects of the annual fundraiser. She combines her traditional training with a connection to spirit and indigenous wisdom. Susan offers individual and group sessions, as well as traditional or customized individual and group rituals.

On a boat adventure to connect with our conscious breathers family, the dolphins ☺

JEN HUTCHINSON - Jen Hutchinson earned her M.A. in Social Entrepreneurship and Change from Pepperdine University, where she focused on the power of girls to create needed, sustainable change on a global level- specializing in the application of the Internet and Social Media. Jen offers one-on-one consultation for girls to design and complete individual projects that impact others, their communities, and them. Jen is also a long time mentor for inner city children in Los Angeles, CA.

MICHELLE HUTCHINSON - Our Logo Designer, Professional Artist, Conscious Consumer Activist, Creative Community Builder and Recycled Art Master has offered her studio as a place for children to: "Experience their own unique gifts in the creative process so they may recognize their place in the universal law of Creation, a place of Possibility and Empowerment."

LEMIA & JOSHUA - Our Amazingly Wonderful NAAM YOGA TEACHERS - NAAM is the yoga of the heart. We work with our Breathing, Body Awareness, Mudras, Meditation and Mantras while Chanting. Gratitude and Reverence are a deep part of this practice.

ED KRAJEC - Our Talented Music Teacher is a former Capital recording artist and has been teaching at the Guitar Shoppe in Laguna Beach for the last 12 years. Having been a mentor to many young people from our community, Ed is eager to share his passion with our I-WE team.

MAGELA ULIBARRI- Our Master Assistant Teacher who raised 5 beautiful children, one very conscious 17 year old, Juliette, who formed "The Conscious Club" in her Laguna Beach High School with over 50 members and is now studying and teaching at UC Santa Cruz.

DEBI MC KEE - Our Crystal Healing Energy Master Teacher who swims and surfs with the dolphins and her 11 years old daughter Lucie who has already offered her help with our younger children this summer. We are so blessed to have them both on the team. Debi specializes in Color whether in Energy or Textiles. With 25 years in Fashion Design, she is eager to teach the concept of designing with the young people at I-WE.

LINDA LEWIS ELBERT - Our Master Cook and Teacher has generously offered her home and amazing kitchen for weekly workshops and summer camp culinary experiences.

JENNIFER MATTOX - Our Master Live and Love in the Raw Chef and filmmaker about Teens and Nutrition, is eager to share her passion with our I-WE students.

CHRISTOPHER SCHECHTER - Our Master Crystal Keeper is looking forward to mentoring our younger generation as he is just out of Massage/Energy therapy vocational school himself and remembers the struggles teens and young people often encounter.

Christopher is involved in various Healing Arts, including Expression through Drums, Painting, Jewelry Making, Dream Catchers and Healing Tools. He is also passionate about teaching History and Science, focusing on the parallels between them and the principles of energetics and quantum physics and bringing skills of sustainable living to the I-WE youth and larger community.

ROSEMARY SEANY - PH.D. - Our Master Macrobiotic Nutritionist and Yoga Teacher is one of our lovely elders. From Germany, she also brings International flavors.

SUSAN TENISON - Our Master Garden Teacher

My name is Susan Tenison. I grew up on a large estate in Jamaica. I employed many people with whom I worked alongside from the age of six. These 'old time' people were my mentors and taught me the subtle ways of nature. I would like to know and participate in any way I can to helping the children of the future stay connected to the land in this rapidly growing world of technology. It is vital we pass on the teaching of the earth that sustains us, the trees that shelter us and give us good air to breath, clean rivers that give us water to drink. This cannot be found by engaging the replica on our computer screen but in the simple act of getting our hands in the dirt together. From the heart, Susan.

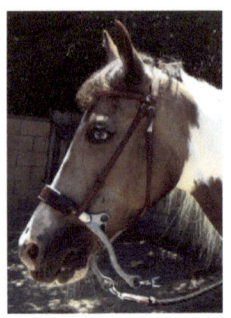

Dixie

Shaylee with Ashley, our wonderful horse lover!

Thank you each, for doing your part in transforming our outdated public education system and for helping to grow new transformative educational models that honor the child first and foremost. I am so grateful for your contribution and co-creation of this I-WE Model!
Satyanna Chris Luken.

ONGOING I-WE COMMUNITY

Every Community has amazing leaders within itself. Your job is to find them and ask them if they are willing to contribute to your children by sharing their passions with them. This is such a huge component of this model. Without it you cannot have an I-WE school. We don't have teachers teaching our children. We only have passionate beings sharing their experiences with them. These people have to be willing to have little shadows follow them at times if an agreement is made between adult and child.

I haven't even shared this with 10% of the amazing people in my Laguna Beach community and already we have many volunteers who are committed to sharing their passion with the I-WE children.

In time, we will be offering teleseminars and podcasts to reach those who are not local. This is the bigger vision for these willing leaders.

There is always Skype, Social media and road trips until we catch up with the technology necessary for the next level of our enterprise!

And, I just may have connected with the right team already because of Green Valentines Festival 2014… More to come soon!

EIGHTEEN LEADERS FROM OUR COMMUNITY SHARE THEIR PASSIONS

Following is a list of some of our community leaders who support the I-WE vision and are presently committed to taking their work into the world. These outstanding individuals have shared a bit of themselves and their passions here, and are available to be contacted directly to support you and your children, in this extra-ordinary, evolutionary, educational journey.

1. Mathematics for the Children of the Future, by Grant Hicks
2. Gardening and Cooking with Children, by Natalia Silva
3. The New Path for Early Childhood Education, by Felissa Silva
4. Public Speaking; From Painful to Powerful, © by Kathleen Petrone
5. The *LIVING YOUR GIFTS*, Girls' Workshop, by Jen Hutchinson and Susan Hough
6. Waking Up the Women of the World, by Andrea Riggs
7. Children as Canvasses, by Rose Wazana
8. Music and Creativity in the Classroom – The Story Behind My Passion, © by Maria Simeone
9. Healing with Crystals & Fashion. by Debi Mc Kee
10. Electrical Engineering (EE) as a Career, by Norm Galassi
11. My Horse Journey, by Ashley Danielsen
12. Kianti's Natural Outdoor Fitness Training Class for Early Teens, by Kianti Murphy
13. Education Transformations ©. by Jacqueline Hicks

14. Learning How to Learn and Being our Authentic Selves, by Ami Sattinger

15. Personal Empowerment Principles, © by Enicia Fisher

16. A Little Child Shall Lead Them, by Dr. Deborah McGill

17. HeartThread and Healing, by Karen Trujillo-Heffernan

18. Where Giving Back Comes Before Art, by Christiana Lewis

Mathematics for the Children of the Future
By Grant Hicks

Having always been fascinated by other dimensions and otherworldly space-time perspectives, and sharing this fascination with so many of the children, I am proud to bring forward an integrated, 7-dimensional mathematical perspective, resonant to the rainbow, our bodies, and the structure of the universe itself. I believe this perspective will revolutionize mathematical and energetic education, liberating people instead of trapping them in mental boxes.

As a matter of fun, I often ask people how they feel about mathematics. The vast majority shrinks away in fear. Most people will immediately start talking about how terrible some part of their math experience was. Some people are so traumatized that they cry when they start to talk about it. When so many either hate math or forget it as quickly as they can, something is wrong with the way we are teaching mathematics. Twelve years of working daily with mathematics ought to produce math masters left and right. We give black belts in Kung Fu for much less work than this, and yet most people feel so inadequate in the face of mathematics.

I love mathematics. It easily expands to realms far beyond the imagination, and yet remains easy to access from the ground up. I enjoy talking about it, playing with it, accessing different levels of its expression, and explaining it. My belief is that making people learn anything they don't want for too long, and then punishing them for not wanting to do it more, is the worst thing we can do to a child's education. The main reason is that they will then hate to do it, and avoid it at all costs later in their life. And if the whole point of making all of our children labor through those years of math is to make us "more competitive" with other nations in engineering and science fields, what a ridiculous situation!

As a means of making mathematics more enjoyable, accessible, and personally relevant, I have developed a system grounded in number and what I call "Universometry."

This system is based on the rainbow, and integrates levels of consciousness, family relations, the human chakra/endocrine system, the stages of a plant's growth, as well as the layout of the universe. In this way, the various dimensions, or levels of infinity, can be seen to be reflected within as well as without, and no longer something outside the grasp of the average student. Within this perspective, students may better orient themselves in relation to the world and the universe at large, rather than being forced to learn things that have traumatized them. The enhanced clarity of perspective, as well as at least understanding the basic unfolding of number and form, in a meaningful context, is designed to increase the appreciation of not just mathematics, but the inner life of the student. This is similar to the way Maria Montessori wanted to bring the world to the children, as they were too small to go around the world and see it all at once. And this is also to emphasize the importance of how the child feels, sees, shares, and experiences the world.

For children of all ages, mathematics has largely become associated with engineering and science, always and only applied to technology and our increased desire to have control over the external environment. However, mathematics is meant to be an understanding of the relations of pattern and order itself. For those parents, teachers, and students ready to access a clear and reasonable, as well as fun and colorful, multidimensional perspective, the rainbow infinity consciousness curriculum is being developed for them.

The gap in perspective between scientists and "spiritual" or "New Age" people has become a cultural challenge that is ready to be met. Scientists typically see spiritual people's ideas as ungrounded or "woo-woo," and many spiritualists consider the ways of science to be far too limited and analytical to adequately express the fullness of experienced reality.

What I see, and wish to teach the children, is a perspective that gives due credit to both camps. The scientists have built their reality from the ground up, and the spiritualists have accessed the realities from the interstellar realms down.

What appears is a full spectrum layout of the many layers of reality, wonderfully developed by such thinkers as Ken Wilber, Plotinus, Plato, Piaget, and Maslow. Great Taoist, Hindu, mystic Christian, modern humanist psychologists and philosophers have recognized that we can explain reality in a great nested chain of being, extending from the densest rock to the subtlest ethers.

In order to do this, it is vital to teach math as forms of expression of the rainbow levels of infinity. This is accomplished by building the numbers up and expanding the dimensions while distinguishing clearly the levels and utilizing Universometry to map out expanded levels of the universe/consciousness. This way the students can understand the motivations to pursue certain levels of mathematics. Through the 7-d system, students see that the math is a function of ourselves, and studying mathematics can be seen to be properly self-reflective, not just used to dominate and control each other and the environment.

Within this expanded, integrated perspective, the students have an opportunity to learn at their own pace, through being excited to learn what is important to complete the next level of their individual craft. Artists need to focus on perspective, rendering multidimensional points of view accessible to the people. Carpenters and architects need access to out-of-the-box designs that reflect the ancient Indigenous ways, as well as the latest new discoveries about geodesic domes and hexagonal or octagonal structures that better support nested communities.

If children were dancing, singing, and playing instruments to learn mathematics, or meditating on sacred geometrical forms, or sewing their traditional patterns, the form and content of the material would have a place to be practiced. As it is, most students become completely frustrated by mathematics, wondering when they are ever going to use it in their future jobs – and few ever need to.

How can we improve the teaching of mathematics and science so that students are more engaged, learn better skills, and have real opportunities to practice their new knowledge?

1. Math and science are fun. When students are allowed to discover how the world works on their own, rather than force-marched through other people's perspectives, they are excited to learn. They want to contribute new ideas and can spend time relishing the wonder of their own enhanced inner perspective.

2. Howard Gardner's multiple intelligences are a key to the way the mathematics ought to be taught. Create a perspective that integrates the visual-spatial, bodily kinesthetic, musical, interpersonal, intrapersonal, linguistic, and logical-mathematical aspects of a child's mind. Also included in this list should be traditional-generational, nature-based relations, and spiritual/universal consciousness. I imagine small groups of students, honoring the feelings of themselves and each other, developing multiple solutions using multiple modes of expression or media, for actual problems the group needs to solve in order to complete the class project. By using words, pictures, and sometimes song and dance, students can integrate all of the Gardner intelligences.

As the entire cultural foundations of our world are shifting, more and more emphasis will be placed on ways of life that honor our inner experiences of love, joy, and community, as well as our true destiny as collective stewards of the Earth and all life forms on it. The indigenous peoples of the world hold keys to this integration process, and their power will only grow as the empire machine crumbles. We need to include the old ways of building, craftwork, dance and music, agriculture, and herbal medicine into our curricula so that future civilizations will know how to live in balance with each other and the wonderful Earth we live on.

The collective fear that most people are living in, which is reliant upon increasingly difficult access to privileged positions within a corrupt and dying system, will be transcended through love and communal vision and action. The sacred ways of our Native people are not lost, though many of the last remaining elders holding lineages are dying.

Our school, including the way we teach science and mathematics, must include ways that honor each other and the Earth we live on, if we are to raise children capable of helping us out of this mess we have created and are all living in.

By giving the students tools to dance, build, nurture, and share with the Earth, the stars, themselves, and each other, in simplicity, beauty, and harmony, we will lay a firm foundation of unity that may be applied within any ethnic or religious tradition. Mathematics and its proper application is a key to this integrated perspective, as it provides access to the map connecting all things. When we access mathematics using sounds, colors, music, and real-time skill acquisition, it's fun for everybody and everybody wants some.

More About Grant: Bachelor's Degree from Trinity University in Mathematics and Philosophy, as well as a Master's Degree in Acupuncture and Oriental Medicine from Texas College of Traditional Chinese Medicine. Also studied Transpersonal Counseling Psychology at Naropa University. He taught high school at McCurdy School in Espanola, New Mexico, with one year each in Mathematics and Science. He taught Algebra 1 to groups of home school students, and has tutored all levels of mathematics up to higher-level calculus for 20 years. In addition, he has led students in after-school programs and summer camps in Lego Robotics, Philosophy, Singapore Math, and Arts and Crafts.

While Grant is developing this curriculum, he is available for tutoring, workshops, speaking engagements, and remote readings with his unique Rainbow Infinity Cards, which provide an introduction to the keys to understanding a universal seven-dimensional perspective.

Grant Hicks can be contacted at: **www.7dhealing.com**

Cooking week with Master Chef Linda

Learning how to flip crepes is so much fun!

Gardening and Cooking with Children
By Natalia Silva

Education and teaching was not always what I wanted to pursue. I contemplated medical school, law school, and business school, all the career paths that we have been taught lead to a successful, happy life. I left my education major program and started taking a philosophy course with the intent of going to law school, of course. I was absorbed in my philosophy classes, and for a year, I relished every moment of lectures and discussions. Then, the daunting realization that this was not what law school or being a lawyer would be about. I realized that Law did not enthrall me, inspire me or captivate me. I gave business school a try, nada. Deep in my essence, my atma, I knew that education was my path, but my mind and fear kept holding me, stopping me. I couldn't be a teacher. How could I be happy living off less than 50K a year? How could I afford to *live*? Then it hit me. I didn't have to know 'how;' I just had to know 'what.' What inspired me, filled me with purpose, and motivated me. Without a doubt, I knew that was education. And I realized that self-actualization, Maslow's peak of self-development, did not depend on your profession or your income. It came from sharing your gifts and love in order to solve problems and help others, while in turn helping yourself. So I enrolled in, and completed, my multiple subject teaching credentials at CSULB. To change and better society through education was my purpose. Cooking and gardening are a necessary means to this end.

I knew I wanted to be in education because of its ability to transform. I believed, and continue to believe, that education is the most effective way to transform individuals, communities and societies. That is why I am a teacher. I have continued to reflect on teaching and its power throughout my career, and I have come to understand that the way we are educating our children simply will not do for the future.

We are educating students for jobs that have not even been invented yet, and a society that will need to increase in creativeness, resourcefulness, and connectedness, if we have any intention of living within the means granted to us by the natural world.

This entails giving up some of our demands for instant gratification and convenience. Our expectations and beliefs must be closely looked at and examined in a context greater than ourselves. They must be observed from a perspective that understands that every choice we make has consequences. Our choices impact our biological, psychological and spiritual wellbeing, as well as the wellbeing of the world around us. Cooking is one way that we can have a deep impact on our families, our community, the globe and ourselves. Cooking, gardening and awareness of the food we consume are skills that have been lost in our culture, to great detriment, and that must be regained.

Some people think, "I have no time to cook, much less garden." We have all heard the expression "Time is money." But what are we buying with that money? What are we losing? We spend such little time thinking or caring about our food that we did not notice the entire food industry shifting right beneath our feet. Our health, the natural resources we all depend on, and our interconnectedness have all been sabotaged. A child does not need a new video game or electronic gadget to develop the skills and attitudes we wish to see as adults. They need our time, our presence and our mentoring. Our children learn culture from us. What culture are they learning if they never experience or participate in cooking at home or school? What are they learning if the only food they know comes from a drive-thru or a box? How do we expect them to care about the environment when their connection to it has been completely obstructed and obscured at a most basic level?

When we garden and cook that connection is evident. We can see the full circle and connectedness around us. We see that the health of the soil is literally the health of ourselves as a species. It is obvious, manifested before our eyes. When we learn to cook from the adults around us, absorbing their knowledge and tradition, we change our relationship with food. Eating is no longer an automatic, unconscious part of our day we robotically go through on our way to someplace else. It becomes a ritual, a place for gratitude and appreciation.

Gardening and cooking help us see how connected we all truly are to each other and our past, and they help us remain connected to those around us, our children, by providing a place to share in such a biologically and psychologically gratifying experience. It becomes part of how we relate to the world. The question is not can I afford to take the time to cook with my child, but can I afford not to?

As a teacher I see the need for this education to take place in our homes and in our schools. We should demand that education prepares our children for the challenges they will face, and the tools to deal with them. To deny our children the culture and skills needed to feed themselves, in a conscious, ethical manner is unacceptable. We must create a new culture of food and eating in which drive-thru meals are not the commonplace and in which we value and respect how we feed each other and ourselves. The experience of a shared meal from garden to table will teach our children more than any textbook or lesson can ever aspire to. We can no longer afford to remove real experiences from our children's education. Nothing is more primal, and evolutionarily bonding, than the experience of tending, growing, harvesting and cooking, in order to nourish the very bodies that house us. In this nexus we can learn how to problem solve, share, plan and create. We can transform ourselves, each other, and the world, through every meal we create, and enjoy together. I used to wonder how I would ever be able to live on less than 50K a year. Now I wonder how we will survive if we forget about our food. ¡Buen apetito!

Natalia Silva can be contacted at: **ms.silva@gmail.com**

The New Path for Early Childhood Education
By Felissa Silva

In 1989, the year I was born, there were 5.23 billion people on earth. Today, there are 7.25 billion. It is estimated that in the year 2100 there will be 10.9 billion people on earth. Along with an ever-increasing population, the amount of energy consumed per person is rapidly growing. Since 1989, energy consumption per individual has increased 20%. Due to our consumer society, the earth's natural resources are being consumed at a faster rate than they are being restored. Sadly, this has lead to the extinction of thousands of plants and animal species, as well as entire ecological systems. These trends are so profound they are changing our world before our eyes.

You may ask yourself, what does this have to do with early childhood education? I say everything. By recognizing our human trends, such as population growth and our hunger for consumption and convenience, we realize that we are faced with the harsh reality of an unsustainable, uncertain future. As educators, faced with the challenging task of preparing our children and youth for what comes ahead, we must not take these statistics lightly.

I believe the health of the planet directly affects the health of everyone, especially our children. If we wish to educate our children well and give them the tools for a better world, I believe environmental education should be the focus of early childhood education and beyond. Exposing children to organic gardening, alternative energy technologies, and the wonders of the natural world, will benefit their development and ultimately the development of the planet. All of these ideas can be incorporated effectively and easily into any program for young children. All that is needed are individuals with a will for progression.

Introducing children to organic gardening will affect their lives forever. Gardening is shown to positively influence physical, emotional, social and cognitive development in children. What better way to teach children healthy eating habits, collaboration, and science?

Bringing nature into the classroom is as important as taking children out of the classroom and into nature. Taking nature walks, field trips to parks and aquariums will foster an admiration of nature in children. This admiration will then grow into love. From love, comes a deep yearning for conservation. This is the beginning of change. Educating children on our effects on the planet will allow for the creation of a new, more compassionate relationship with us and all other life. This is my goal for children, education, and the planet.

Felissa Silva is an honors baccalaureate graduate of the Child Development program at California State University, Los Angeles.

Felissa Silva can be contacted at: 949-351-8659.

Public Speaking; From Painful to Powerful
By Kathleen Petrone © 2014
President & Founder of the Academy for Public Speaking

We are not born afraid to speak. We cry and freely express our emotions as we enter this world. As infants, we watch, listen, and interact to learn what words mean. When we finally speak our first word, it is extremely powerful - a cause for celebration! Our parents smile and cry as they are moved to tears by this amazing milestone.

Words can be wonderful. We express our love, our gratitude, our compassion and our concern. Yet words can also be used as weapons. The power of the spoken word can be precious and priceless or piercingly painful.

For many adults, public speaking is our number one fear. But it is not actually the act of speaking words that most people fear. It is the reaction that may result. It is the fear of humiliation or rejection.

As a child, I was a happy, outgoing, and expressive little girl. I was comfortable with who I was and extremely confident. But then one day in third grade, I received devastating news. It was my greatest childhood fear. I found out I had failed the eye exam. I would have to wear glasses.

It wasn't that I actually feared wearing glasses. I feared the reaction that might result from wearing glasses. I feared humiliation and rejection. I feared being made fun of and called names such as four eyes. I was even afraid my best friend wouldn't like me anymore because I decided I was no longer a "cool" kid.

My self-esteem was shattered. I became so uncomfortable with myself I did not want to speak. I was afraid to speak because of what might happen next. I didn't want to draw any unnecessary attention to myself for fear of being made fun of by my classmates. I wouldn't even make eye contact with my teachers.

I was a smart kid who almost always knew the answers teachers wanted, but that didn't matter. If a teacher called on me, then everyone would look at me and that would be so embarrassing!

The reality is I let my fear stop me and control my life. But why did I do that? I was the only one who decided I was unworthy. I don't actually recall anyone ever making fun of me, and my best friend didn't disown me. What I did develop from this fear of judgment were some negative behavior patterns such as not expressing myself verbally, being indecisive, and being unassertive. These bad habits negatively affected my personal relationships, and they limited my professional life too.

Despite my fear and negative habits, I became a happy and successful adult. I was close with my family and friends. I graduated from college, became a classroom teacher, and owned a nice car and home. Yet my life wasn't the best it could be. When I met the man I wanted to marry, I knew I would have to take a risk and learn to express myself verbally and emotionally. I decided to confront my fear, take control, and make a change. I decided to develop my confidence, assertiveness, public speaking, and leadership skills. Though I was terrified, I joined Toastmasters. This was another major turning point in my life. Although I didn't know it at the time, I was also acquiring the skills I would need to become a successful entrepreneur a few years later once I discovered my passion and purpose in life.

I have always been passionate about teaching children, but I frequently question what, why, and how we teach children in our public school system and how much time we spend on assessment. Cursive and penmanship? Memorization and regurgitation? Multiple guess tests? We often omit essential skills such as communication, financial literacy, and applying knowledge to solve problems. Can you imagine how different and much better off our nation and our world would be if everyone was schooled in communication skills, financial literacy, and solving problems? Thankfully, the Common Core Standards are beginning to address our severely outdated education system.

Being comfortable with who I am and expressing myself has not only freed me from fear, but it has also given me a special gift I now excitedly share with children and adults who may be holding back and limiting themselves in life due to a lack of confidence. No matter what goals a person decides to pursue, having confidence and effective communication skills will help him or her achieve those goals and live a happier, more successful life.

In 2010, I founded the Academy of Public Speaking to help children become confident, effective communicators. We offer fun interactive courses and private coaching sessions to help children from second grade through high school and adults creatively express themselves as they develop confidence, public speaking, and leadership skills. Contrary to many public school systems, our programs focus on learning by doing, actually applying concepts and skills, and experimenting with new techniques rather than just constantly assessing students with tests, tests, and more tests. Through performance-based education, our students learn to provide written and verbal evaluations for their peers in a positive, helpful, and friendly manner. Students receive an abundance of immediate feedback from their peers and teachers, including both compliments and suggestions for improvement. Academy students also learn the importance of respect, compassion, and cooperation. One of the most important lessons our students learn is their participation, opinions, and advice are essential components of the education process.

In our first 3 years, the Academy for Public Speaking empowered over 700 students to become confident, effective communicators and leaders who use their voices to inspire others and improve our world. Our graduates have also reported numerous personal benefits from our courses such as improved listening, speaking, and writing abilities, feeling more confident, giving more powerful presentations, and earning better grades in school. Graduates of the Academy for Public Speaking have not only improved their relationships with themselves, their friends, and their parents, but they are also less likely to be bullied. Our graduates have experienced the empowering feeling of being in control of their fear, speaking before peers, leading a meeting, and presenting their final speech project to a large audience, including parents, teachers, and peers.

Children who can confidently and creatively express themselves are happier, and they have an advantage in school and life. Give your child the gift that lasts a lifetime – the gift of confidence!

Public Speaking Success Stories - From Painful to Powerful

Little Tricia sat frozen in her seat with a deer in the headlights look on her face. I had just introduced Tricia to share her first speech before a small group of her classmates. Tricia was a sweet, quiet, and very well behaved fourth grade student. I could tell Tricia didn't feel comfortable sitting there in defiance of my expectation for her to go to the front of the room and share her speech. The notes on the table indicated Tricia was prepared, but she was not ready to risk speaking. Tricia didn't move except for shaking her head slowly, slightly back and forth. Her sad, scared eyes sincerely said it all. "No, I'm sorry. I can't speak right now."

This had never happened before so I wasn't sure what to do. Then remembering my own childhood experience of how I couldn't stand to have everyone looking at me, an idea suddenly came to me. I said "How about if we all look away and you just share your speech from your seat?" Tricia nodded so I quickly said, "Okay, everybody look away," and I promptly modeled looking up at the ceiling.
The other students had fun following my lead. Everyone looked at the ceiling, the wall, or through the window while Tricia sat in her seat and shared her speech. At the end of Tricia's speech, we all applauded. I felt so proud of Tricia and myself for thinking of an idea that worked.

At the end of class, Tricia approached me and asked what I wanted her to do for the following week. I had not planned to have Tricia present a speech during the next class, but then another idea came to me. "Tricia, how about sharing that same speech from the front of the classroom next week?" She smiled at me and said okay.

The following week Tricia shared her speech from the front of the classroom. Tricia improved tremendously throughout the course, and she taught me even more. The final speech project for our level one course is a persuasive charity speech.

Tricia's mother runs a non-profit organization so Tricia chose to represent her mother's charity. During rehearsal, Tricia's classmates and I heard her speech for the first time. We thought it was really sweet that Tricia chose her mother's charity, but then Tricia's speech became emotional in a way we had not expected. Tricia shared, "My mom spends so much time on her charity helping other children. I am jealous, and I wish she would pay more attention to me."

We were shocked, yet amazed at Tricia's sincerity. What impressed me most though was the metamorphosis from the extremely shy girl who had been afraid to get out of her seat and speak during her first speech to the clearly confident girl who now, just six weeks later, stood before us freely expressing an emotion she had formerly suppressed.

During her graduation Tricia won the persuasive charity speech contest and a donation for her mother's charity. Tricia realized the lesson I hope all children learn. Your voice is a powerful tool you can use to make a positive difference in our world. Your voice and your words make a difference - in your own life, in the lives of those you love – your family and friends, and in the lives of other people throughout the world.

Since graduating from the level one course, Tricia has participated in the advanced class and competed in a few speech contests. Tricia has also appeared as a special guest speaker during several of our free introduction classes to share her inspirational story from living with a fear of public speaking and expressing her emotions to freely sharing her feelings and living a more confident and happier life.

Tricia's story will always hold a special place in my heart since she was the first student I helped overcome extreme anxiety. However, there have been other students we have also helped since Tricia. While I was observing one of my instructors teaching a pre-teen class, she encountered a similar problem with a third grade boy named Tim. Tim actually went to the front of the room when he was introduced to share his first speech. Tim had his notes, but he just stood there staring at us.

Despite the teacher's supportive and encouraging prompts, Tim silently stood frozen in terror looking petrified and feeling too scared to speak. The instructor glanced over at me questioningly so I began trying the technique that had done the trick with Tricia.

Unfortunately, this technique did not work with Tim. When dealing with individuals and helping them overcome extreme fear, there is a process of trial and error involved to discover what will work for that particular person. For Tim, the technique that worked was letting him share his speech with me one on one after class. The following week, Tim finally shared that same speech from the front of the room.

One of our sixth grade students, Cassandra, was thirty seconds into her first speech, when she began crying and ran out of the room. Cassandra was so scared to come back and give her speech that she skipped the next class. However, with some extra support Cassandra overcame her fear and presented her first project from her seat. For her next project, Cassandra spoke from the front of the room. During her graduation ceremony, Cassandra's instructor and I proudly watched as she confidently shared her persuasive charity speech in front of a large group of her classmates and their parents.

One of the best benefits of teaching children confidence is the ability to change a child's life. During one of our after school enrichment courses, a second grade student named Adam refused to come to the first class. Since Adam's parents knew our course could help him overcome his fear, Adam was reluctantly escorted into the second class by the school's childcare supervisor. Adam looked mortified and was visibly upset. The supervisor sat with Adam in the back of the classroom to give him time to calm down and observe the environment. Adam just watched us that day.

At the beginning of the third class, I saw Adam standing outside the door peeking in through the window. I invited Adam in and he sat next to me. As the course progressed, Adam intently observed all that was occurring. He always felt safest in the seat next to me and although Adam didn't speak much during his first course, he learned a lot.

Even though Adam had what would be considered a slow start for most students, it was exactly what he needed to overcome his intense fear. Now Adam has participated in our level one class twice, and he has also completed the advanced class.

I remember how rewarding it felt when Adam finally found the desire and the courage to speak. As Adam shared his first speech from the front of the room, it warmed my heart to see how patient, supportive, and proud his classmates could be. In these extreme cases, these children actually seemed afraid to speak. Can you imagine living life this way?

If you have a fear of public speaking, think back to your childhood. What was your turning point? When did you become afraid of what might happen when you speak, and why? Are fear and anxiety affecting and limiting your happiness and success?

What about your child? Is your child afraid to speak in class or in front of a group of peers or adults? Do you wish your child seemed happier, more confident, or had more friends? Do you worry about your child being bullied? Would you like your child to be a confident, assertive leader? Do you wish your child had better listening, speaking, and writing skills and higher grades?

If your answer is yes to any of these questions, our public speaking courses can help your child. Although the majority of our students begin the level one course feeling nervous to some degree, children who are already confident also enjoy the challenge of creatively expressing themselves and being in control during the classes.

For me, the key to becoming a successful entrepreneur and a happier person has been becoming a confident leader who views public speaking as a powerful tool rather than a painful event. Our graduates have applied their skills and experienced success from winning scholarship money by competing in speech contests to achieving positions of power in student government and on speech and debate teams to successfully interviewing for admission to private schools and colleges.

What are your child's dreams? Does your child have the confidence and communication skills to do whatever his or her heart desires? Set your child up for success. The Academy for Public Speaking transforms public speaking from painful to powerful & gives children the gift that will last a lifetime – the gift of confidence!

To learn more about the Academy for Public Speaking, please visit **www.AcademyforPublicSpeaking.com** or contact us at **info@academyforpublicspeaking.com**.

© 2014 Kathleen Petrone,
President & Founder of the Academy for Public Speaking

(**The children's names have been changed to protect their privacy.)

The *LIVING YOUR GIFTS* Girls' Workshop
By Jen Hutchinson and Susan Hough

The *LIVING YOUR GIFTS* **Girls' Workshop** is a transformational empowerment program for young women, ages 8 to 11, and 11 to 14, designed to:

Guide girls to develop their intuition, to construct proper boundaries, and to live with integrity.

Empower girls by examining how the framework of gender norms/roles are created and reinforced- by the media, education, and peer relationships.

Inspire girls to begin a life long journey of self-care, self-growth, and personal achievement- as women.

The name *LIVING YOUR GIFTS* was inspired by African Author and Spiritualist, Sobonfu Somé', and the Dagara cultural and spiritual life of her native Burkina Faso, West Africa. There it is believed that each person brings a needed GIFT into the Village, for its health, prosperity, and sustainability. Here in the U.S., our 'villages'- our communities and families- are fractured, and the media manufactures a damaging culture for women and young girls. *LIVING YOUR GIFTS* is aligned with the worldwide movement recognizing women and girls as *"the most powerful force for change on the planet."* At *LIVING YOUR GIFTS,* we understand this to mean that the 'global village' is calling in women's and girls gifts now- *for its health, prosperity, and sustainability.*

Research shows that girls self esteem plummets around age nine, in disproportionate amounts to same age boys. Psychologists note it is conflicts "between the psychological needs of females and society's gender-role expectations, as girls learn from their families, school and the media which behaviors are approved." Social norms are institutionalized, internalized, and then self enforced, with external costs beyond the individual girl.

LIVING YOUR GIFTS was created to specifically attend to the needs of young girls in Orange County, CA, who following national trends experience mental health issues such as anorexia and bulimia, and the associated effects of low and loss of self-esteem, such as premature drinking and smoking, and lowered academic achievement.

At ***LIVING YOUR GIFTS*** we do not believe it is a coincidence that in indigenous cultures around the world, girls at this age undergo communal, guided initiations and rites of passage. In *our* society 'initiation occurs whether we want it to or not. When we don't understand this, we end up creating unrelieved suffering.'

Cheryl E. Czuba, facilitator of the People Empowering People Program, defines empowerment as "a multi-dimensional social process that helps people gain control over their own lives." In the ***LIVING YOUR GIFTS*** Girl's Workshop, we seek to utilize some indigenous ways and means as a novel approach (in Western culture) to relieve the suffering caused by the 'self esteem epidemic.' We work to create a clearing- outside of media, of patriarchy, of peer pressure, and non-functional family dynamics- as a space for deep transformational healing, growth, self-discovery and self-empowerment that is lacking in modern Western society for young girls.

"The first requirement for empowerment is to understand that power can change. The second requirement depends upon the idea that power can expand." The transformational ***LIVING YOUR GIFTS*** curriculum, offers an opportunity to create and experience change in how norms operate or influence our lives, which can lead to changes in peer and other relational group behavior. The activities in the Girl's Workshop are hands-on, engaging, and relevant to participants' own life experiences, and our program incorporates consistent mentorship, positive role modeling, supportive peer groups, interactive teaching methods, gender specific programming, and experiential education.

The ***LIVING YOUR GIFTS*** Girls Workshop

"Girls tend to feel fine about themselves when they're 8, 9, 10 years old but they hit adolescence and they hit the wall." Jean Kilbourne, Killing us Softly, Advertising's Image of Women

LIVING YOUR GIFTS was specifically created to address what can be called the 'Self Esteem epidemic' among young girls in the United States. Studies by the American Association of University Women, the National Association for Self Esteem, and the Center for Substance Abuse Prevention find that girls' self-esteem erodes dramatically between fourth grade, when they are eight or nine years old, to the time they enter junior high school. In fact, girls' self-esteem drops off two times as much as boys in adolescence, and statistics now show that girls are seven times more likely than boys to be depressed, and twice as likely to attempt suicide.

Researchers link these conflicts between the psychological needs of females and society's gender-role expectations, as girls learn from their families, school and the media which behaviors are approved. Social norms are institutionalized, internalized, and then self enforced; and the external costs are not borne by girls alone. Tamara Woodbury, the CEO of the Girl Scouts—Arizona Cactus-Pine Council, perfectly describes it when she says that today in the U.S., girls are "being socialized to underestimate their value."

In school, "though girls talk, read, and count earlier than boys, score higher on IQ tests in pre-school, and are ready for formal schooling at an earlier age, by eighth grade girls report more negative self-regard and self-confidence in behavior, and characteristics such as perfectionism, hopelessness and discouragement rise with age.

The American Psychiatric Association has linked girls' low self-esteem to media exposure. "By the time a girl is 17 years old, she has received over 250,000 commercial messages through the media. Young women see more images of beautiful women in one day than their mothers saw through their entire adolescence."

The amount of time that adolescents watch soaps, movies and music videos is directly related to their degree of body dissatisfaction and desire to be thin. In the last 20 years, the incidence of anorexia nervosa, which stems from psychological distress, has doubled, and is now presenting in Kindergarten. Other associate statistics reveal that 81% of 10 year olds are afraid of being fat, and the number one wish for girls 11-17 is to be thinner.

"These are all public health problems that affect us all, and public health problems can only be solved by changing the environment."
-Jean Kilbourne, Killing us Softly: Advertising's Image of Women

It has been shown that "75% of girls with low self-esteem engage in negative activities, such as disordered eating, bullying, smoking or drinking." Researchers find that the risk of suicide by adolescent females has the potential to add $280 million to $350 million to the costs of adolescent obesity and premature mortality costs. And in a world where one in six women experience interpersonal violence, in the U.S., victims loose almost 8 million days of paid work...equivalent to more than 32,000 full-time jobs, and almost 5.6 million days of household productivity."

At **LIVING YOUR GIFTS** we do not think it is a coincidence that in indigenous cultures around the world, girls at the ages of 8, 9, and 10, undergo initiations, rituals, and rites of passage. Not only have we lost connection to this (healthy, mentored life transitioning) in the West, we have missed the associative benefits to individuals, and to our culture- *and* we have created an alternate mythology around these concepts, relegating them to taboo status.

"When we left our indigenous tribes, we gained much in the way of individual freedom, but we lost much of our understanding of the necessity of ceremony and initiation...we still require initiations, rituals...so that we may grow into conscious individuals." -Karla McLaren, The Language of Emotions

Traditionally, "tribal initiations are performed as a way to guide members through life's transitions. Tribal societies create a container and a foundation from which all growth and transition can be understood and overseen." The most basic initiation or rite is characterized by Mythologist, Michael Meade by the following three stages:

- Isolation or separation from the 'known world.'
- The experience of an ordeal or trial.
- The return/welcoming back of the initiate.

Meade not only stresses that each stage is crucial to the whole, but also, that all phases must be completed for the transformational process to occur. In our society 'initiation occurs whether we want it to or not, because it is a necessary passage in our lives. When we don't understand this, we create unrelieved suffering that we try to hide in intellect-only, spirituality only systems.' Or, what can be especially correlated to young girls and the "Self-Esteem Epidemic;" when the welcoming tribe is composed of similarly traumatized people, initiates get the wrong message about belonging and identity, and many healing and recovery tribes don't foster a deep connection to our larger society or culture as a whole. Instead...one becomes a survivor of a specific set of circumstances instead of becoming a fully initiated adult."

OUR PROGRAM

In essence, girls are currently 'initiated' into a world of dysfunctional gender norms, upheld by institutions and culture, and they are experiencing the related hardships. ***LIVING YOUR GIFTS*** uses the three step initiation process as a "container," a term developed from Cognitive Anthropology; an abstract perceptual object which consists of an *interior*, *boundary*, and *exterior*- to create a space *outside* of the 'known world' of media, of patriarchy, of peer pressure, and non-functional family dynamics, as a clearing for deep transformational growth, self-discovery and empowerment. At issue is the fact that girls in our culture do not undergo the third step. LIVING YOUR GIFTS Girls Workshop seeks to provide the structure for this step.

- Through discussion, exercises, and experiential learning, we deconstruct and remove girls from their "known world" of skewed, institutionalized, self-internalized, and self-enforced gender norms; for example: from the Media's image of what is "supposed to be," and from their 'tribe' of negative peer reinforcement. We create and hold this as *"sacred space,"* where it is understood that each girl will be truly 'seen,' and she will be supported, and related to, as her true self, by all present.

Empowerment is a process that fosters power in people for use in their own lives, by acting on issues they define as important.

- Within this 'new' container, we go inward to re-experience and examine our personal wounds from the low self-esteem epidemic. And we explore using some ritualistic elements as part of the multi-dimensional approach to empowerment. We develop intuition (our internal GPS) to find and experience our own true ways of being. Within this space, boundaries are discussed and formed, and healthy choices, decisions and leadership are enacted.

- "Empowerment is a process that is similar to a path or journey, one that develops as we work through it. One important implication of this definition of empowerment is that the individual and community are fundamentally connected." We 'welcome the girls' back into a collaborative, mentored community, with supportive peer recognition. This community extends to our online community where girls can continue to be supported, to experience, and to act as 'their true selves, with self-empowerment and civic opportunities. And where they can experience seeing other girls and women achieving and thriving as women.

INSPIRATION *"Our tribal selves still live inside us, and our ancestral DNA has hundreds of thousands of years of indigenous memory that competes with a mere handful of hundreds of years of modern life." -Karla McLaren, The Language of Emotions*

"There is a deep longing among people in the West to connect with something bigger — with community and spirit." - Sobonfu Somé

LIVING YOUR GIFTS was inspired by the work of Sobonfu Somé, and the indigenous Dagara Cosmology of Western Africa. A fundamental belief is that everyone brings a vital GIFT into the village that is needed for the health and prosperity of the Community. It is the tradition that the women gather with the pregnant mother, and listen to the child speak the GIFT it is bringing in. This will become a part of the child's name, and the community will nurture the GIFT until it is ready to be contributed.

Sobonfu's name means "keeper of the rituals," and ironically, as she was growing up and learning what her GIFT would require of her- traveling the world to spread indigenous wisdom- she resisted it, because she did not want to leave her village. Sobonfu's GIFT was nurtured through teaching, ritual and mentored community support. Today, she is the author of three books, and is considered the foremost expert on African spirituality.

Living Your Gifts has synthesized this inspiration, (please see below for the co-founders' backgrounds, work experience and education) into the following vision statement:

"In the indigenous culture of Burkina Faso, West Africa, it is understood that everyone brings a needed GIFT into the Village, for its health, prosperity, and sustainability. Here in the U.S., our villages; our communities and families, are fractured, and the media manufactures a damaging culture for women and young girls.

LIVING YOUR GIFTS is aligned with the current worldwide movement that is recognizing women and girls as the most powerful force for change on the planet. We understand this to mean that women's wisdom, energy, and contributions are being called in for the health, vitality, and prosperity of the GLOBAL Community NOW."

Susan and Jennifer can be reached at:
http://www.livingyourgifts.com

Waking Up the Women of the World!
By Andrea Riggs

My name is Andrea Riggs. I am a trial lawyer turned holistic healer. How you ask, does one make the leap from a career based on logic to one based on heartfelt healing and intuition? Well, I used to help people sue others over what they were angry about. Now, I help them with what they are angry about so they don't have to sue anyone.

I am also an inspirational author, speaker and workshop facilitator. My first book *Wake Up, American Women* was published in 2011. I wrote it because I grew up believing that women in America had always enjoyed the multitude of freedoms and choices that were available to me. Of course, I'd heard of Susan Anthony, but she was just a blip on a radar screen, a single paragraph in a history book. One woman, one life, and one paragraph made all of women's historical contributions appear easy and effortless. There was no mention of struggle or strife.

After starting law school in 1990, I heard repeatedly that mine was the first class to have more women than men. I didn't realize at the time what a remarkable achievement that was, even though it was a mere 51%, just barely above half. Unbeknownst to me, a woman attending graduate school was just becoming fashionable.

When I practiced law, I was the only female attorney working in an office with five men. I wasn't aware that most of the women just one generation ahead of me had been limited to the careers of secretary, nurse and teacher. Nor did I understand that their sacrifice and efforts made it possible for me to sashay into my profession of choice.

I left private practice for a position at an international Fortune 500 company. I was in my mid-thirties and finally beginning to track some of the patterns that had appeared in my education and short career. It was here that I finally began to understand the long-term, devastating effects of the unconscious messages about body image and marriage expectations on women.

All around me were women in their early to mid-thirties shifting into an absolute panic about not being married. Beautiful, bright, funny, financially independent gals who had the world at their feet were falling apart because they were not fast tracking to the white picket fence. None of them were basking in their career achievements or pondering the vast world of opportunities available to them. No. Each one was asking the same question: "What is wrong with me?" Studies showed me that seven out of ten women ages fifteen to sixty, avoided meeting friends, exercising, voicing an opinion, attending school, going to work, dating, or seeking medical attention because they didn't like the way they looked. That was just the tip of the iceberg. Current statistics show that 97% of all girls tell themselves at least 13 self-deprecating messages a day.

In addition, the web site www.mindonthemedia.org gives the following statistics:

- 80 percent of ten-year old American girls, diet. The #1 magic wish for young girls age eleven to seventeen is to be thinner. (Remember when the #1 magic wish was to have a pony or ride a magic carpet to Disneyland?)

- Females cite the media as the most important source of pressure to be thin.

- Studies show that reading "teen magazines" and seeing only thin models creates lower self-esteem, body dissatisfaction, decreased confidence, and potential eating disorders.

- By age thirteen, approximately 53% of American girls are "unhappy with their bodies." For girls aged seventeen and older, this percentage rises to 78%.

These shocking statistics, along with anti-depressant use doubling in the United States over the past decade, sent me on a five-year journey of research.

Why are the women and girls with the best circumstances in the world feeling so lousy about themselves and how can we turn this trend around so that they can be leading the rich lives that are abundantly available to us?

I found my answers in the healing arts. We do not need diets, surgeries, invasive procedures and countless products to assist us. We need to stop repeating the patterns of the past and change the way we are feeling on the inside. We need to re-discover our worthiness and our wholeness. We need to find our unique gifts and talents so that we may share them with others. We need to use our voices, step into leadership and make the contributions that will bring us back to a place of partnership and balance on our planet.

The Dalai Lama predicted at the 2009 Vancouver Peace Summit that Western women would save the world. With all of our freedoms and privileges comes responsibility. We have the tools and the techniques available to us to become happier, healthier, more conscious individuals. With the expansion of our own consciousness we can raise the vibration on our planet.

My goal is to give our girls the tools they need to lead happy, healthy, productive lives at their full capability and potential. I look forward to this time of exploration and expansion. Together we can make the world a better place.

To purchase books you may visit my website at: **www.wakeupamericanwomen.com** or go to: Amazon.com at: **http://www.amazon.com/Wake-Up-American-Women-Threaten/dp/1450293840/**

For more information or to schedule an appointment or event, you may contact me at 949-229-5434; PO Box 1361, Newport Beach, CA 92659; or visit my website at: **www.wakeupamericanwomen.com**

To be inspired and add your voice to our conversation, please join us at: **https://www.facebook.com/WakeUpAmericanWomen** and **www.meetup.com/AwakenedWomen/**
NAMASTE!

Children as Canvasses
by Rose Wazana

I have been very lucky to be teaching art for twenty years now (and counting), both in the private sector as well as public. We all know that the arts have all but disapeared in the public schools, as music and other valuable creative expressions. As I reflect on my teaching philosophy, I am deeply humbled, awed, and so very grateful by what "I" have been taught by my students over the years. My teaching style has certainly developed, changed, and morphed into this symbiotic relationship with my students.

In the past it was all about the principle, the concept that I was trying to convey to them. I had a "goal" in mind. These blessed days my approach is more relaxed, organic, letting things unfold. My lessons now can take a turn in an instant, and I go with it! Inspiration is certainly the springboard, while allowing for creative expression is at the heart of all that I do. When children are given carte blanche to be fully in the moment of their own creations, they shine. I have watched students' temperaments change, I have witnessed their faces when an "aha" moment occurs, a calm quiet awareness replaced by angst, or an excitement over a new medium they have discovered! I see a process through an experiment, which they are the explorers of their own inspirations. I realize after so many years, that yes, I am an art facilitator, yet I am so much more, I am also ultimately a bridge! I lay a foundation of trust and give permission to all my students to fully allow them to BE themselves! I hold that space for so many children to "feel". This feeling, when nurtured, becomes a space they can always tap into; a well that can always be accessed. It is their own reservoir built by their own volition. The best part is they can apply this expression to math, science, or language. What an epiphany that was!

Children are naturals. They have an instinctive understanding of the world around them. They are connected to a sort of magic, and if we adults can allow that natural unfolding to take place, we can be part of that wonder and magic. I believe it is vital to their self-esteem as well as their self-empowerment.

Art is also a healer. In my own personal journey, I have understood that creating is the one thing that I have always been able to rely on. Through tragedy, disappointments and upheavals, or through the best of times, that space is always there, waiting for me. If I can give one thing to my students, it would be that! To realize that space of creating is always waiting for them too. This outlet can be their sacred protector. A haven that allows for a time to reflect on themselves. Perhaps they too will become bridges and give permission for others to do the same. Educating my students has had a profound humanistic rendering of myself. It's as if they hold up a mirror to me and say "take a good look Ms. Rose!". I have realized the ominous responsibility of my work. We are growing children! And by teaching my students to value art, I teach them to value all that is around them! Trees, plants, oceans, animals, people, the land, the sky, the world! I hope to inspire them to learn to see the magic that is always around them, and in turn, it is a constant reminder to me.

I encourage them to be curious about the divinity in nature, the divine symmetry in a shell! And then they get to paint it, draw it, or construct it!

Somehow I know they already have a keen intuitive knowledge, a deep reverence for the natural world around them. I am just at their side guiding them through what they deeply understand. My perception of my work has unfolded into this realization that I was meant to do the work I do, that I was given this opportunity to not just educate children, but to open them to their own beautiful process, and to rely on their own best selves. Art is the medium, and they truly are the canvasses! The journey has been the best gift and I am still on the road paving new grounds for new eager faces, their shining eyes looking at me with wonder and excitement. Not a bad way to start my day.

Rose is an Art Instructor/Educator/Healer

Rose Wazana can be contacted at:
rosewazana@yahoo.com

Music and Creativity in the Classroom - The Story Behind My Passion © 2013
By Maria Simeone

IBM recently polled 15,000 CEOs across the Nation who identified CREATIVITY as the #1 "leadership competency" of the immediate future. Yet, current demands on teachers and administrators leave little time for "creative pursuits" and exploration – let alone time to reflect on the experience! What can be done, when there is such a seeming disconnect? How can we realistically prepare students for the 21st century's "conceptual age" while meeting current benchmarks? How do we motivate students to think creatively when they've predominantly been trained to "find the one right answer"? To explore the possibilities, we need to look at the nature of creativity and the role music plays in stimulating our innate imaginations.

Initiating Creativity in the Classroom

The process of creativity involves the ability to formulate *multiple questions* with *multiple answers* (called divergent thinking). When we settle on the best combination of these solutions (called convergent thinking) and they have value, we call that "creativity". So first, to cultivate this innate skill, we need to encourage students to ask lots of questions! Fortunately, this is a natural capacity. The average preschooler asks 100's of questions throughout their day about their world and how it works. But, by the upper-grades, many of these same children have learned to stop asking. When the questions stop, disconnect occurs. Students become disconnected from their own thoughts, opinions, and passions. Passion is the fuel of creativity. To reignite their inquisitiveness, we need to provide a safe and supportive environment so that they feel it's safe to ask lots of questions – questions that are meaningful to THEM. We initiate their inquiries, by encouraging students to come-up with questions that are connected to their immediate environment, their immediate experiences.

This exploration can take all of a few minutes at the beginning of the day. (These short sessions also provide ample material for future lesson plans!) We can and should use music to prep the environment prior to these question/reflection sessions, as the right music has the power to turn resistance and hesitancy into openness and willingness. Music that is familiar, with a steady and consistent beat can deactivate the brain's "fight or flight" response – the resistance some students may communicate when presented with a new challenge. The right music, played softly, will relax the mind and body, and students will automatically become more willing to participate. While there are many nuances to choosing the right music -- music that is purely instrumental, played softly at a moderate "walking speed" is particularly helpful. Native American drum music can suit this purpose and gives students the grounding pulse so many students need, in order to settle their thoughts and organize their systems. In classical music, the "second movement" of concertos or sonatas from the Baroque to Classical music periods is another good option. "Second Movements" of Concertos (Vivaldi, Bach, Corelli) or Sonatas (Mozart, Beethoven) at a slow- moderate walking speed with simple orchestration or a single instrument (strings or woodwinds) are best. This music will quickly bring everyone to the same state of relaxed alertness. Relaxed alertness, or what is also called the "alpha state", is the optimal state for new learning, problem-solving and creativity. It's the brain-wave state we most want to support in the learning environment.

Exploring Creativity

The day begins and your students enter the room with music (as recommended above) playing faintly in the background. As they become situated you pose a "what if" or a "what do you like to do best" question. You pass-out UNLINED paper and softly shift the music to that which is "creativity-inducing". Options include: instrumental ONLY jazz, movie soundtracks, world music, music with variations (such as Mozart's variations on the French "Twinkle Little Star" melody) and orchestral "program music" (e.g. music that tells a story via the instruments).

"Creativity-inducing" music is characterized by both spaciousness and complex, changing rhythms. These characteristics spur the creative mind. Program music, due to its storytelling nature, evokes vivid imagery. Imagery, symbols and metaphors are the very language of creativity. Therefore, this type of music is a direct and reliable stimulus. In addition, the music's texture brings a sense of novelty, inspiring natural exploration. By having students brainstorm on <u>unlined</u> paper, in a <u>non-linear</u> fashion – they are more accurately mirroring the pathway of the brain's creative thinking process—one that is *circular* in nature. This circular process supports the brain's <u>actual</u> form and function.

The momentum in the music will continue to motivate those who "can't think of anything else." The imagery/symbol nature of the exploration will support those whose creativity is often stymied by worries of spelling, punctuation or even the physical demands of writing itself. Like all great inventors, scientists and musicians, the "best (creative effort) is often last." So, encourage students to **fill** their papers with ideas and images knowing that the music will bring them **deeper and deeper** into their endless imaginations. The process can also be easily connected to the day's teaching concept. This divergent thinking activity, which can be done in as short as 5-10 minutes, will engage students with meaning and purpose for the day's lessons.

<u>Sharing Creativity</u>

Deep learning happens most profoundly in <u>groups</u>. Therefore, after the initial brain-storming, have students share their ideas in pairs or small groups. In their small group, students combine their <u>collective</u> ideas into **best solutions**. "Aha!" Pupils have now created something of value derived from their <u>own</u> imaginations! This "Aha!" creates its own "music" in the brain. Dopamine (the motivation chemical that says, "That was rewarding! Let's do it again!") is secreted and we have just reinforced a very positive learning experience, <u>intrinsically</u>! In addition, this satisfying process happened within a social context, reinforcing camaraderie in the classroom.

This bonding potentially reduces or even eliminates future behavior problems. Students are now connecting to their passions, gathering support for their ideas and working as a team. They are collectively reigniting their creativity through music.

Our Students and Their Future

The rules of intelligence are changing. Creativity, divergent thinking and innovation are all becoming the differentiating factors in today's world. These differentiating factors are also crucial for a resilient and successful life. Students who have cultivated an active imagination become adults who are better adjusted, have healthier relationships and are more optimistic about their future. Music plays a key role in this evolution into adulthood. Music is a way of learning about all of life, and is an ongoing gift we need to give to all of our students. Through music, our students, as well as ourselves, can learn more deeply, feel more profoundly and connect with one another more meaningfully. Music is the very link to our humanity. Through music, we can inspire students to imagine a future filled with creative solutions to the world's problems and to create healthier options for day-to-day living. Through music and our endless imaginations, life becomes richer and sweeter. It meets us wherever we are at, and brings us joyfully to our full potential.

The Story Behind My Passion
Copyright Maria Simeone

My passion for arts-integrated, child-centered education is truly a passion of the heart – the roots of which are found in my own childhood. Furthermore, this fascinating journey brought me to a revelation about my own public school experiences. As a child, I would devise elaborate plays, songs and dances – not realizing at the time that this was learning at its most authentic level! By contrast, traditional school had taught me that "real" learning was "hard work" not to be confused with "play" (and certainly improvised music and movement were play)! I accepted this for a long-time, while remaining stubbornly committed to my music and dance (outside the classroom!) knowing innately that it was a necessity for healthful, vibrant living – and NOT simply the "icing" on an otherwise dry academic "cake."

It wasn't until adulthood, that I began to consciously integrate music/movement "play" within the process of my own learning. It made a dramatic difference and caused me to question the old educational paradigms of "serious school work" and "play," as separate entities. Indeed, I was discovering that the opposite was true! Learning and creativity were powerfully intertwined! As a parent and teacher, I became an advocate for exploratory, child-centered learning that integrated the arts. I found this strategy to be universally effective for ALL children regardless of labels, economics, or prior experiences. Arts-integrative learning that was child-centered and exploratory did the most good for the greatest number of children. One of the significant "results" being that children unleashed their own intrinsic motivation for learning!

Not surprisingly, this journey led me to become soberly aware of how antiquated our educational methods had become. Learning is the most naturally human activity we can engage in! It's simply astounding that our school system, on average, has managed to make learning effortful and joyless for the vast majority of children! Music programs are removed in the primary grades when it's the most critical for their development. Children are expected to sit for far longer periods of time at far younger ages, when learning via movement is the most natural. Many of the "extracurricular" music programs that do exist, tend to focus on product, competition and performance (often in an effort to justify their worth!) rather than process and child-centered play! Throughout my twenty-five year educational career, and as the mother of two children who've overcome significant challenges themselves, I have NEVER met a child who does not want to learn when given the creative tools with which to do it! I HAVE met many children (and adults) who have NEVER experienced effortless learning and who have finally given-up. How many brilliant, creative minds have we lost as a result? Learning through the arts is the answer for these children and for all children because it is innate to our very development.

Through my work, I'm convinced (and there's now a plethora of scientific evidence to support my conviction!) that the reason music/movement based learning is so universally powerful is due to our "first relationship" – the relationship that sets us up for our entire life. That first relationship is the innately musical womb! What we all know from our womb experience is rhythm and movement. What we also know is that this fully integrative experience (magnified via the baby's watery environment) is done in personal, intimate relationship. When babies are born, they know the timbre, rhythm, nuance and resonance of their mother's voice! They know the songs that were sung to them, the music the mother listened and moved to during pregnancy! THIS is where we find the roots for profound learning. Even if the mother never sang to her child or listened to music – the orchestration of her vital organs resonating in synchronicity with her child, is its own music as the baby's systems form and develop! Why, the vary shape of the brain is that of the human ear! Quite astounding when you think about it! Therefore, NO amount of technology can ever compete with the profound learning that can come from an artistically rich education experienced in meaningful relationship with others! However, even more important than a child's academic development, is the character and compassion that develops through such meaningful learning. There is no high-tech substitute that can teach that. Meaningful, relational arts-based learning gives life profound joy and limitless purpose that has the power to spread to the four corners of the Earth. This is the real educational legacy I want to leave my children, all those I play with, and those still to come.

Maria Simeone can be reached at:
http://musicmovesthebrain.com

Healing with Crystals and Fashion
by Debi Mc Kee

I worked with Satyanna for a few years teaching at the I-WE school in Laguna Beach, CA. I was honored to be able to work with sweeties from ages 2-14. We covered many subjects, including: Fashion Design, Intuition, Crystal Energy, Crystal Healing & Meditation, Ocean & Water Awareness.

Working on these various subjects gave us the opportunity to expand on each subject that one would not normally get to relate to. Intuition was definitely a key to opening all other creative forces. Our environment at I-WE was so very open without restriction or lines and walls to suffocate us on the intuitive arts and spirituality.

I initially started the children with Crystal Energy awareness and their minute properties & geological origins. They were able to hold 10 different Crystals and learn to feel the differences in the pulses and temperatures in their hands and body parts. Where do you feel it? What does it feel like?

We played intuitive games such as holding a crystal and guessing its color. Having each child sit back-to-back and guess/feeling what the other had in his/her hand. One might get pictures, feelings, sensations, colors or animal pictures in their minds. There are no wrong answers, just different interpretations. It was fascinating to see! We all sat in a circle and one by one they felt the stone's energy and shared what they saw with one another.

We ended the week's studies with the children lying on the floor while they all put four of their favorite crystals on their Chakra points. I asked all the children to breathe into their Chakras, with the different colored crystals and describe the sensation. I waved the healing Selenite wand, white light and Universal Energy, with the Crystal Energies on them. It was all very relaxing and tranquilizing. Every child needs to come home from school feeling like this!

Each morning from 9:00 AM to 12:00 noon, we would meet down at the beach for some water play, ocean awareness and a nature scout. Experiencing tide-pools and discovering treasures on the sand were part of our daily routine. Teaching the children about wave height, riptide patterns, water temperature and nature's flow is imperative to squish the fear out of the ocean's existence. We would do a small meditation listening to the surf's pounding on the sand right before lunch. This was my kind of recess! No smelly and dirty black top, but healing sand! No choosing sides, just jumping in! Being aware of your surroundings, checking safety, then relaxing and enjoying the surf!

The last month of the summer included "Fashion Week." I introduced them to conceptualizing their own clothing line. They came up with a name (graphic design), concept of images and whom they would sell to (line concept & demographics). They designed flat sketches and individual clothing pieces (design board), picked out fabrics they liked and how they would use them (textile design and merchandising), then did a presentation of the whole kit and caboodle (sales presentation).

They all had fun and surprised themselves on what they could do. It sure brought out their personalities, deep confidence and natural achieving abilities. When they were designing and working with the textiles, after asking them so much about 'how does that make you feel?,' they were very comfortable in sharing that!

Interestingly, if they were a shy child who had a bit of trouble expressing themselves, when it came to choosing their colors and pieces, they 'knew' better what they wanted to do. Teaching them to trust their innate instincts and intuition to run their world and feeling confident in their decisions.

I would love it if the world of learning adapted these concepts in regular schooling. It teaches Nature's way of the senses and it is absorbed so very much more simply into their souls.

Crystal Swirlies, Debi Mc Kee is a 4th Generation Healer, Native of Southern California. A.A. in Textile and Merchandising, B.A. In Fashion Design, 3 Year Degree @ I.C.I. Institute of Denver Colorado, 23 years experience in the fashion industry worldwide (which was ALL about color), 15 years' experience in Crystal Healing Energie' Certified by Melody in the Laying-on-of-hands Method, Reiki II Master, Pranic Healing, Medical Intuitive, Mah Jong Cards, Astrological Charts, and Past Life Regressions. Color, Design and Balance Consultant for the purpose of healing one's heart, body, home and soul.

Debi is a Crystal Energie' Healer
and Holistic Health & Wellness Practitioner

Debi Mc Kee can be contacted at: 949-496-0989

http://meetup.com/Lemurian-Crystal-Energy-Workshops-by-the-Sea
facebook.com/debi.mckee13

http://www.CRYSTALHEALINGENERGY.COM

Electrical Engineering (EE) as a Career
By Norm Galassi,
Instructor in Electrical Engineering, CSU Chico

Why might YOU be a future Electrical Engineer?

>Do you like to solve puzzles?
>Do you like to take things apart to figure out how they work?
>Are you fascinated by invisible things that happen, such as:
>>Why does cling wrap cling?
>>Why do my socks stick to my shirts when they come out of the dryer?
>>Why does a compass point north?
>>Why do magnets attract or repel each other?
>>Why do I get shocks when I open doors on dry winter days?
>>How does radio work?
>>How do lights and motors work?
>>What's with those wires that come into my house?
>
>Do you love to do math problems?
>Do you think a lot about how things work?

What do Electrical Engineers do?

> Electrical engineers use their knowledge of the invisible electric and magnetic forces to create products and services that make our lives safer, healthier, and more fun.

Most products that you use in your daily life have some electrical engineering that makes them work or work better: Radios, TVs, microwaves, blenders, Lights, computers, refrigerators, heaters, air conditioners, automobiles, & so on.

> A lot of products you rely on but don't necessarily think about also contain a lot of electrical engineering in them: the power grid, GPS satellites and receivers, lots of medical instruments MRI, EKG, X-ray, machines, even digital thermometers and digital blood pressure instruments.

What kinds of classes do Electrical Engineers take?

> Core courses in math (like algebra, calculus, & more); Physics (basic physical laws); Chemistry (more basic physical laws); electric circuits (ordinary magic); electronic circuits (almost fantasy); and electro-magnetism (very mysterious stuff).
>
> Also specialized courses in computer logic, computer programming, and esoteric stuff like how to send and receive information (communication theory) and how to make machines work safely & efficiently (control theory).

So, why did I choose to be an Electrical Engineer?

> When I was 9 or 10, I spent evenings listening to radio programs (in the days before TV) and remember wondering how radio worked. About the same time, I remember watching the city workers put up strings of Christmas lights as well as linemen putting up power and phone lines. I thought that would be fun.
>
> Later in my early teens, I took radios apart to see if I could figure out how they worked. Mostly I killed the radios. Later in my teen years, I became interested in amateur (Ham) radio and spent hours listening to foreign radio programs and Ham operators all over the world on an old radio that was used during World War II to communicate between Army Air Force air planes.
>
> In high school I loved my math, physics and chemistry classes, joined the radio club, hung out with other "radio guys," and absolutely "knew" that I had to study electrical engineering … it was my hobby and I was passionate about it!

So, how did that work out for me?

I got summer and part-time jobs at Hewlett Packard (long before HP became a computer company) that supported me during college. After graduating, I joined HP as an Electrical Engineer and had an amazingly wide career:

1. Started in semiconductor device (diodes) processing (mostly chemistry)
2. Went on to design semiconductor test equipment (in the days before computers)
3. Moved on to design computer controlled test systems (lots of programming)
4. Joined HP's new computer operations (lots of hardware and software design)
5. Spent a few years in marketing ... process control systems for manufacturing
6. Rejoined the HP computer operation ... BIG high performance computers (not PCs)
7. Towards the end of my career I developed internet based products (lots of software)

The bottom line: I spent 40 years "doing my hobby!"
After I retired, I was given a fantastic opportunity to teach electrical engineering classes at Chico State University – now "I teach my Hobby!"

I am also still doing my hobby as an active Ham Radio operator and "home brew" equipment designer and builder ... a lifetime hobby and career as a definite GEEK!

The bottom line for you is this:
It really pays to follow your passion whatever it may be!

My contact info is below, and I am glad to correspond with anyone desiring to go deeper on the subject. Norm.

email: norm.galassi@gmail.com
email: nrgalassi@mail.csuchico.edu
Phone: 530 513 2244
snailmail: Norm Galassi, PO Box 7155, Chico, CA 95927

My Horse Journey
By Ashley Danielsen

My fascination with horses started before I could talk. My mother and grandmother would take me to the public library where I would pick up anything with a horse on it. I remember admiring their vast bodies, strength, power and unbridled freedom. Recognizing my passion for horses, my mother wanted to help me explore it further. She began to research horses, horses and children, and horseback riding. She was able to locate one program that allowed kids under the age of eight to be around horses along with other farm animals at the local college.

At the ripe age of four years old, I was enrolled at the local college for the farm and 4-H program. On the horse day, the instructors took us on a tour through the barn. What I remember most was the smell: something of leather, dirt, sweet grain and carrots. This quickly became my definition of fresh air. As I breathed in the amazing aromas I spent time observing horses in their stalls, in turnouts, alone, and with other horses. I was amazed while I watched them play with each other by shifting their bodies, jumping up, stomping their hooves, and even scratching each other's backs with their teeth. I thought to myself at that moment that the horses were just like me. I liked to run, jump, play with friends, relax and sleep just like they did. I was so grateful to be in their presence, they brought me such peace and happiness.

At ten years old, after completing two years of weekly lessons at Butte Creek where I learned how to groom, tack, ride, clean stalls, waters, and bathe the horses, I competed in my first horse show and was able to begin leasing a horse named Cowboy. Cowboy was my sole responsibility for three days a week. I gained so much confidence from spending the extra time with the same horse. The best part was the bond. The first time 'Cowboy' whinnied for me I nearly cried with pure joy. I felt a true sense of love, compassion and companionship.

Horses are more like human beings than even dogs. Just like children they do not like to try new things that make them feel insecure. But, once they have learned it, they love to do it, and to share it with everyone. Horses are also more compassionate with the young children than the older ones as they see them in images like a baby horse. During the lesson, we will do things like a treasure obstacle path, keeping the child's and the horse's minds occupied, to overcome their fears and master their skills.

I began my first job with the horses when I was fourteen. I was asked to teach my trainer's daughters to ride and in exchange, she offered to help teach me how to break and train my first horse, an Arabian named Czar. I spent countless hours at the barn working with her daughters and my new horse. It took a while to forge the bond that I had achieved with Cowboy but when I did I had a great sense of accomplishment.

At sixteen, I was asked to show other Arabian horses that were in training to help increase their value for resale. The job was presented to me as a way to be able to afford to take my own horse to shows, so I took it. I learned all about horse shows, the schooling show level, and then the much harder shows the class A level. I was able to braid other horses' manes and tails for my class entry fees, which was how I was able to compete with Czar. I showed both schooling and A circuit Arabian horse shows until I graduated high school.

After graduating high school, I made my way to southern California and reestablished myself at a barn in Laguna Niguel exercising young horses in need of training. I was able to work with the horses on the weekends, while going to work and school during the weekdays. It was the best of both worlds. For a long time, I worked real estate and focused on the horses on the weekends, until I was laid off in 2004. I then had some time to reevaluate what I was doing in real estate, as I knew that my place was with horses. It was then that I began researching other local barns and found a small one in Huntington Beach that didn't have a trainer. I was able to make contacts and help people by riding their horses, and teaching them new techniques.

I began teaching lessons there, starting with the children of my friends and asking them to spread the word if they liked what I was able to teach. By word of mouth only, my business grew thirty percent in the first year. By the second year I had enough clientele to quit real estate all together.

At first I thought I would just give back the gift of pure happiness and joy of being around horses. However, I shortly came to the realization that through horses, the kids were learning to be compassionate towards animals and others. They were learning to stand up for themselves at the barn, in the classroom and at home. They were feeling accomplishment by way of meeting a goal with the horses, which in turned helped their confidence level. Their social skills were improving. Grades even improved for some of the kids. The horses and I were working together to teach the kids that it was okay to be afraid at first to try something new and that it's okay. to be curious and take it slow; really the ultimate goal is to reach success even if the way there is a slow process.

In my work over the past 10 years with both horses and children, I have come to realize that they are very much the same in how they learn and what they like. Both horses and children see and learn in imagery. This is especially true for autistic children. In the seminal work of Dr. Temple Grandin, herself diagnoses as autistic at age 3, she has shown that the same things that calm animals, such as slow, deep touch, will also calm the autistic child, as well as children with ADHD.

Such things as swaddling or her padded "squeeze machine," which emulates the restraining walls between which livestock is held to calm and hold them, work well on children who might otherwise react negatively to being held.

The effect on autistic children, all children, really, of a calm and gentle horse is profoundly comforting, as well as being a wonderful means of drawing an introverted child out of their shell. My newest autistic child is doing amazingly! He started just six weeks ago, riding in tandem with me, frightened to even pet the horse. He's now trotting on his own, having so much fun!

Horses teach children social skills...don't ask me how, but they do. I have every child I teach help groom and get the horses ready for their lesson and also give them a treat at the end of it. This provides a strong bond and shows the horse that the child is willing to care for them. And the horse learns from this to care for the child.

The way I work with my horses is by the way of connection, not fear. Horses want to work with me and not because they fear me, unlike the way other trainers use force and fear, as well as having only one way to teach and work the horses, such as Western style. We include grooming, the vaulting (gym on horse back), bareback riding, trails, and English and Western riding. By combining all these varied techniques and approaches, no one gets bored; not the horse, nor the child. We need to teach our children like this as well, with a kind and patient variation of styles and activities. It's not right to "break" a horse. And it's not right to "break" a child, either.

This is my wish for the world:
That we would find a way to peacefully communicate with each other in the way horses and children communicate naturally.

For more information please contact:
Ashley Danielsen
ashleydanielsen@gmail.com
All About Horses OC, LLC
949.228.2183

Kianti's Natural Outdoor Fitness Training Class for Early Teens
By Kianti Murphy

Kianti's Natural Fitness classes begin with the more stimulating environment of the outdoors, a classroom without walls, with a lot of room for play! I believe that it is crucial to keep our youth active to overcome our country's obesity epidemic. The more they participate in play, the greater their overall health. My class is about being physically active, however I am teaching them while on the field and in our stretching circle. My program is designed to create individuals that know how to and are inspired to take excellent care of their health. Beginning at a young age propels them through life with greater ease. My students take with them lessons that they can use every day and that will last for the rest of their lives.

I began my work with children by avoiding accounting class. Instead, I chose the route of home economics, preferring to learn woodworking, cooking, and how to care for children. In high school, I took a child daycare class where we watched, entertained, and educated sixteen preschoolers. Before getting into teaching, I did some part time coaching of high school wrestling. My first teaching jobs were for the Creative Learning Place and the Emerson Academy where I taught classes in environmental education.

While at California State University, I joined an environmental club on campus where I began speaking about how to better care for the earth. In a nutshell, I have become a school teacher by taking my passion for helping others through public speaking, and combining it with my passion for improving relationships, especially with our planet, and have developed my curriculum around the healthy planet from a healthy body and mind circular model.

My fitness class reinforces that being a team player increases their abilities for thinking how their actions affect others. Additionally, they benefit from sharpening coordination, mental focus, and increasing their lung capacity. I help them increase their balance, mobility, strength and agility with speed.

My version of physical fitness training incorporates a focus on nature that relates each human to a spiritual awareness of spatiality and how to move through life in a way that will serve and protect them well. In this creative space, I connect my student's fitness thinking to their ecological relation to life. I remind my students to stretch up into the sky like a tree, reaching up towards the atmosphere looking through their hands, noticing whether they see a cloud or a bird or a plane. In my fitness class, I weave other personal growth and training methods geared towards emotional self-monitoring and control. This is practiced and reinforced by including Tai Chi and elements of meditation and spirituality with an ecological thread relating to our natural environment. During stretching and Tai Chi I teach them breathing techniques, stress reducing exercises, moving meditation, and the power of visualization to put in their superhero tool belts.

While I teach all kinds of people, my program is geared for preteens in home schools and private schools. I find it especially rewarding to teach children with learning disabilities such as Autism and Asperger's Syndrome. These boys and girls are gifted with highly intelligent minds accompanied by social disorders that require a personalized approach only available in private or home schools. They may become some of our greatest problem solvers, thus securing a better future for our planet.

Not coincidentally, I can relate to them. I had a really tough time learning math as a child. My memorization skills were slow to develop. My teachers put me in a special needs class for a week, but I preferred to struggle through much of school rather than be labeled 'retarded'. I eventually went back to college to get my bachelor's degree in interpersonal communication studies. I've pushed through my learning challenges, having developed ways to focus my brain. Being an outdoors physical education teacher seems to be my calling, as I have found that teaching suits my challenge of being 'a differently-paced-person,' while the outdoors is my preferred classroom.

Kianti's Natural Outdoors Fitness Training Classes include fun and interesting Tai Chi sessions where I invite the students into a circle telling them variations of the story of how the first version of Tai chi was developed around thirteen movements simulating animals. I ask each one to offer up an answer to questions like, "Which is your favorite move or animal and why?" My students take away the understanding that Tai chi is for maintaining emotional balance, relieving stress, for finding calmness, and clearing our minds in difficult daily situations.

It took me a long time for this Renaissance man to sort through all of my talents and interests. I've found teaching to be what I do best having my greatest impact. My students like me, and I like it that way. I show them care and respect. I serve to be an example of how they should be. I enjoy saying things to them like; "Don't be too hard on yourself. Be patient & keep on trying. Never give up the things you really want in life and the things that you know you are really good at! Now go out and change the world!"

Kianti Murphy
Ambassador of Good Will
Kianti Murphy can be contacted at:
Phone: 818-455-6597
Facebook:
https://www.facebook.com/Kianti?fref=ts

Education Transformations
By Jacqueline Hicks

Education Transformations was born out of my strong conviction that relationship skills are essential and fundamental to the learning process. Everyone wants to be heard and understood. Sadly, most school classrooms are too often painful places of no one being heard or understood. Not the students, and certainly not the teachers. Over the years as a teacher, educational counselor, and founder and principal of a comprehensive charter high school in downtown San Diego, I have enjoyed a great deal of success in my relationships with people of all ages—particularly people whom others find difficult. I can see the breakdowns in communication between teacher and student, student and parent, parent and teacher, and teacher and principal. I see the pain caused by communications made that are not being understood, and how futile it is to keep talking when no one is truly being heard. Of great concern to me is that the results of painful communication and misunderstandings can lead to bullying, scape-goating and even violence in school, and in society as well. I am committed to helping educators develop relationship skills that they can also teach to their students—skills for transforming conflicts, suspending judgments, and eliminating blame. The following article shares some of my experiences dealing with violence in school.

School Violence and What Constitutes a Safe School?
By Jacqueline Hicks ©

Students report that clear plastic backpacks, metal detectors and armed guards in school do **not** make them feel safer. They feel like prisoners in their own school. So what does it mean to feel safe in school? It is easier to say what makes school feel unsafe: physical abuse and violence, verbal taunting, ridicule, threats, spreading rumors, and humiliation, all of which can now take place more publically and to a much wider degree, thanks to modern technology. Cell phones, texting, YouTube and Facebook now allow us to torment each other instantly worldwide.

Most students have been both perpetrator and victim to some degree of these behaviors in the course of their school careers. So we all are capable of making someone else miserable and know what it feels like to have it done to us. When students don't feel safe in the school environment, classroom, lunchroom, playground, corridors, restrooms, stairwells, after school waiting for the bus or on the public transportation to and from home, they can't fully engage in learning. They are either preoccupied with an earlier incident or thinking about how to avoid a future perceived torment.

Most adults believe that the older the students are the less they need (or want) adult help. It isn't true. Even adults have difficulty dealing with bullying and intimidating behavior. Just look at our U.S. Congress. The older we get the more serious the intimidation can become. Dealing with bullying in school at every grade level requires adult (particularly parents and teachers) involvement.

How can elementary school children deal with the playground bully? What happens when children fight back? Or tell an adult what's going on? What happens when they don't?

My wisdom about the answers to these questions comes from my own experiences as a child, student, parent, teacher and school administrator. What I've learned is that adults are generally ineffective and unreliable in dealing with bullying behavior. They wait too long to address it. They encourage kids to "ignore the bully, s/he will soon get tired of it and stop." The old adage, "Sticks and stones can break my bones but names can never hurt me" is just not true. Words and name-calling can be very hurtful. Often both bully and victim, receive the same punishment. We suspend and expel them both, which does not prevent the bullying behavior from happening somewhere else with more fear and anger. KIDS NEED HELP FROM ADULTS WHO KNOW HOW TO DEAL WITH THIS VERY SERIOUS ISSUE AT SCHOOL.

I've learned what doesn't work; I've also learned what does. No one--administrators, teachers, parents and certainly not students--can deal with bullying on their own. So much of the time, as is often reported after the fact, the adults claim to have been unaware until the worst happens, while students claim that the behavior took place right under their noses. They want us to see what's going on and do something about it and they are not comfortable to tell us directly because what we do about it doesn't work.

Some things that **have** worked and why….

Situation #1
When my youngest son was in 4th grade Special Education, he and some of his classmates were regularly tormented (taunting and physical pushing and shoving) by a playground bully. This had been a topic of discussion with their teacher in class. No effective solution had emerged as to how to deal with the situation. My son is a very peaceful person who avoids physical conflict while confident in his ability to defend himself, which he gained from his study of karate. He and his classmates had taken too much of the abuse, finally one day at lunch, my son pushed back and knocked the bully down. His classmates were backing him up and looked on cheering. In their eyes my son was a hero. No adult witnessed this playground fight, so he and the other boy were not punished for fighting. The teacher, who knew from her class that this student was bullying them, shared with me that although she didn't condone fighting, in this case she was very glad that my son stood up to the boy on behalf of himself and his classmates. I believe this worked for my son because he and his classmates had a **rapport with their teacher**. She and they had discussed this problem looking for a solution. When my son took matters into his own hands to settle things, **he wasn't alone**; his class was with him and his teacher understood that **natural consequence** is a strong teacher. However, what happened to the student who was doing the bullying? I do not believe anybody followed up with a plan to positively integrate this boy into the school community. **I believe he remained an outsider who would continue to bully other students.**

Situation #2
My oldest son, when he was in 7th grade, came home from school one day complaining that for the last several days his lunch was being stolen out of his backpack and he had been going without lunch. Although he had a suspicion about who was taking it, he wasn't completely certain and he didn't want to "squeal," which he perceived as having unpleasant consequences; and since he didn't know for sure who it was, there wasn't much the school would do about it. My kids really enjoyed their sack lunches brought from home and lovingly packed by their dad, so eating the cafeteria lunch was not an option. My husband, son and I were able to craft a creative consequence that took care of the bullying without tattling. The plan for the next day was a lunch packed and left in the backpack with a few extras—some Tabasco sauce poured liberally on the sandwich, cayenne pepper sprinkled on the chips and the usual juice box was not included this time. In addition, my husband would drop off a real lunch for our son in the office before lunchtime. The spiked lunch was stolen that day, and that was the last time my son's lunch disappeared. **However, the bully was never discovered and the problem remained unaddressed by school personnel.**

The following two examples are from my small public high school that was based on a person centered approach:

Situation #3
Several juniors had been with each other since ninth grade. They had been through my leadership program where they learned about and practiced congruence, empathy and unconditional positive regard. A student joined the school in the middle of the year – a bit of a loner, someone who didn't know how to join in and relate to the other students. He and his family enrolled in our school because of bad relationship experiences elsewhere. He came to me and shared that he was getting some harassing phone calls at home (he wouldn't tell who), and his parents were also very upset about what was being said on the phone, which is why he brought it up to me.

As Counselor of the school and the person who enrolled this family, I had made some promises that we deal directly and effectively with things like this. With his parents' encouragement, he finally told me who was phoning him. I was very surprised at who was doing the bullying – kids I perceived as very inclusive. I called them into my office and asked why they were tormenting this student. They said they didn't understand his odd behavior. They attempted to befriend and include him. When he didn't respond the way they thought he should, they started teasing him, just trying to 'get his goat.' I explained that he and his parents were very upset and I asked them what they proposed to do to 'clean up this situation.' They and he all agreed to a meeting facilitated by me. They all wanted to be friends, and just didn't know how to get the other's positive attention. The discussion that took place was very effective because they all listened to each other and began to understand each other at a deeper level. They were willing to be real with each other and take responsibility for their actions, even the new student. I concluded that the reason it was so effective was because the students had a background in leadership development, personal responsibility, person-centered approach, and they had a relationship with me that they valued. They were able to use the skills they had been taught to transform the conflict and be authentic with each other.

Scapegoating goes hand in hand with bullying. The dynamic is about wanting attention—any kind of attention. A student who becomes a scapegoat is used to, and even comfortable with, everyone's anger, thinking s/he might even deserve this cruel treatment. Such a student is sometimes very aware of the things that really bug other people, seeming to purposely push everyone's buttons. S/he starts out the day planting negative seeds with the other students and their teachers as well. Then throughout the day s/he goes about watering the seeds and by the afternoon, an entire garden of upset has emerged. The scapegoat then becomes the recipient of some mean and cruel reactions. A bully might find a scapegoat the perfect target, and others in the community will think she deserves it. An example:

Situation # 4
A Russian student called Katya was teased mercilessly and didn't have much savvy about American culture. Much of her behavior was born of fear of her past situations and imaginings of what might happen. She became a scapegoat for some of the other students who found it difficult to accept what they thought was paranoid behavior. She often accused other students of talking about her behind her back and plotting against her. Even her teachers became weary of her complaints and sometimes hysterical disruptions to their classes. One day her hair was burned with a lighter by a classmate. Katya ran from the room and took a couple of other students with her to provide comfort. It was a major disruption to the class and other classes as well.

When breakdowns occurred in class, it was our practice to have the entire class form a circle and to focus on the feelings, thoughts and information about what was going on, until we get to the bottom of the upset. Some of the students knew who had done the deed, but were reluctant to tell. I went to work with Katya. The teacher reminded everyone about what kind of school they wanted, what behaviors were hurtful and what needed to be done to create the kind of school community the students wanted for themselves. With encouragement and persistence, the student who lit Katya's hair on fire finally admitted that she, Donna, was the culprit. Donna shared her hostile and frustrated feelings about Katya. Other students shared some of the same feelings but did not condone the action she took. The class was able to have an honest, open conversation with Katya after their group process and my individual work with Katya. Donna and her mother and I found another school placement for Donna. The students in Katya's class, including Katya, learned some things about assumptions, judgments, and overlooking bullying behaviors. They found out that they could talk about things that bothered them and that the adults in the school would be there with them. Katya's relationship with her fellow students began to improve that day and she was able, eventually, to make some real friends. I learned those who are the hardest to love, need it the most.

What makes a school feel safe is:
- ➢ An environment of open communication and respect among students, teachers, administrators and parents.

- When someone's got a problem, we take time to deal with it.
- Everybody knows your name.
- Less competition and more collaboration.
- Students, parents, teachers and visitors alike feel welcome on campus.
- The presence of Person Centered Approach (PCA).

In my experience, the elements of a safe school are achieved best when there is a high degree of personal development among the staff. When people know how to relate to others using congruence, empathy and unconditional regard, the number of painful and unsatisfying interactions decreases significantly. People stop blaming others when problems arise; listening with the intent to understand becomes common practice; appreciation for the differences among students and teachers is prized; and communication becomes efficient, allowing the business of teaching and learning to go forward without fear

What are congruence, empathy and unconditional regard?
I like to describe congruence as an authentic sharing of my experience, thought, opinion, belief, or feeling as far as I understand myself in that moment. Empathy is my willingness and my ability to be completely present with another while they explore their experience, setting aside my own feelings in order to follow them on their journey. For me, unconditional regard is openness to the potential that exists between us, and treasuring the differences another brings to our relationship in that moment. These are the core attitudes of the Person Centered Approach. They are very necessary to create a safe school.

School safety is often very little about physical safety and mostly about emotional safety. If students feel that they can talk about anything that concerns them, and teachers feel free to engage their students authentically, then the community they create together will be a safe and peaceful place.

Learn more about Jacqueline Hicks and **Education Transformations** at: **www.edtrans.org**.

Learning How to Learn and Being our Authentic Selves
By Ami Sattinger

Learning has been my greatest joy and my deepest challenge throughout my life. In fact as a young child my last name was Lerner, until my mother remarried and my stepfather adopted me. I became more aware of this strong message from the universe as I began tutoring high school students when I was in college, and felt great satisfaction helping them with lessons that had been difficult for me. I was extremely intuitive as a young child and was acutely aware of the thoughts and feelings of others. Unfortunately no one would talk with me about my sensitivity, and I was often ignored and discounted if I tried to talk about these experiences.

I was able to function moderately well in some aspects of my early childhood education and elementary school, however as soon as math and science became more difficult in middle school, I began to struggle with these linear subjects. When I entered High School, I was still able to function in the liberal arts and social science type classes; however math and science became more and more difficult for me. I was given permission to drop out of Geometry after being unable to improve with a tutor, and never took another math course.

Once I entered college the pressure intensified, and I began to realize that I could not succeed in the standard mold of the academic world. Instead I began looking for experiential courses that would offer me an opportunity to learn by doing, rather than through learning a theory, and I had a bit more hope that I might be able to graduate.

I began working as a social worker, and was able to connect easily and create resources for our clients when they needed assistance. After a few years, I left the field and began to study Astrology. Within one year, I became a Professional Astrologer and began working with people of all ages. My inability to learn Geometry had been transformed as I practiced Sacred Geometry in my new career.

The first thing I realized as an Astrologer, was that the most challenging patterns in a person's birth chart often held the key to their greatest gifts. My job was to provide the love, compassion and creative solutions to support each person to become their authentic selves and share their gifts with the community.

I wanted to support families through Astrology, and realized that if parents could accept their own personal challenges, and find creative solutions and support, they could be present to support their children. As I began doing the children's readings, the parents were more open to acknowledge the talents, gifts and challenges their children were dealing with in their individual birth charts.

I remember doing the chart of a very bright eleven-year-old boy whose parents were getting divorced. He began playing with some Legos and cubes while we were talking, and I asked him if he ever felt that he had a "brain in his hands". He instantly understood what I was talking about, and began to relax. In his chart he has a particular pattern of someone who has a great deal of ability to use his hands, which might be expressed by taking toys or other things apart and putting them back together again. Fortunately his parents were both educators and recognized this special gift of his, and encouraged him to develop it. As an adult, it might translate into someone who is good at sculpting clay, being a hairdresser, a designer, or even being a body worker or energy healer. These people have an incredible sensitivity and creativity when they use their hands in these different forms of expression. If they don't channel this energy, they might end up worrying too much or analyzing everything in their lives, thus blocking this tremendous creativity that they possess.

I was excited to be able to acknowledge each client's learning style as illustrated through the patterns in their birth chart. When I did children's charts and they were in middle school or high school, I would talk directly with them about some of their gifts and talents, and then address their challenges involved with learning. Since there are usually one or two ways that a child or adult learns information, I would discuss the different ways such as visual, auditory, kinesthetic or sensory, as well as olfactory, in a very simple way to acknowledge them immediately.

Once they felt I understood them, we would discuss ways they could use their talents and gifts to their best advantage. In addition I provided simple strategies to help them overcome their challenges in certain areas, and encourage them to use their personal astrological timing to their best advantage. I have often used the example of different voices or parts of our selves, as being represented by the different planetary energies in the charts in a lighthearted and humorous way. This helps most people to relax, and see that its perfectly okay to have these different parts, as long as we are able to use them in a positive and loving way towards ourselves and others.

Another part of my gifts involves my own love for storytelling, improvisational theater, puppetry, stuffed animals and voice acting. Since I was a child I have always treasured my stuffed animals, or stuffies, and would share my secrets with them. As an adult, I had continued to have a small collection of stuffed animals, and they began to take on a new life after my work in improvisational theater and voice acting. Soon after my creative training in these two areas, I returned to work with children as a tutor, and a nanny, and found myself taking my two favorite stuffies in the car to play with the children. What had begun as something rather fun and entertaining, began to serve as a way to heal and inspire the children.

My two stuffies were very different in size and personality, a small charismatic Lion, named Leo, with his fur almost worn down (much like "The Velveteen Lion") and a large round hippo, named Gertie, that gave hugs and encouragement to the children. I would take the stuffies with me everywhere. When I was working with the children, I found that they became a source of comfort and joy for some, whereas other youngsters rejected them, and were sometimes unkind towards them.

These experiences allowed me to see the power of the childlike heart and to recognize which children were more in need of emotional nurturing and support, than academic tutoring. One of my favorite children had a brother that was about ten years older than him, and felt more like an only child.

He embraced both stuffies in a powerful way and we could not even drive anywhere unless he and the stuffies had their seatbelts on. Lucas also encouraged Leo to eat more vegetables and fruits, instead of a diet of chocolate cookies. In addition, he and the two stuffies would go on imaginary adventures to save the world. Lucas would talk about it in endless detail when we were out driving somewhere, or at home playing together. It showed me the power of love and imagination that Leo and Gertie could evoke through their generous hearts and spirits, and the importance of my holding the space for it to happen naturally, with each child on our path that we encountered out in the world.

I am excited to combine my work in Astrology with my magical stuffies, to help the I-WE children learn how to learn, in a joyful and creative way, and empower them to be their authentic selves, no matter how old they are.

Ami Sattinger
www.AstroCoachAmi.com
Cell: 949-235-9793
ami@astrocoachami.com

Personal Empowerment Principles
By Enicia Fisher

The Element School's program is based on seven Personal Empowerment Principles, which serve as a guiding philosophy for our students, community, and learning environment. These Principles are incorporated into the development of curriculum, are referred to in our workshops, and offered as affirmations for application in a student's daily learning adventures. They are based on the wisdom teachings of many global faith traditions.

1. I am pure, infinite **Potential**.
2. I am **Creativity** in action.
3. I am the expression of **Freedom** and **Purpose**.
4. I am original **Individuality**.
5. I am **One** with nature and all humanity.
6. I am the presence of positive **Consciousness**.
7. I am **Complete** and **Self-Fulfilled**.

PHILOSOPHY

Education at The Element School focuses on the personal growth of each individual student. Our philosophy is that learning is a facet of personal growth, and personal growth is a facet of learning. We believe learning is an innate desire that must be nurtured, protected, and cultivated. Learning is a lifelong, natural process, enhanced by an ecology of learning that encompasses social, emotional, and spiritual development; integrates the personal interests of each member of the community; and enriches the individual and group like a lovely permaculture garden in which each individual element thrives by its relationship to all of the combined elements.

"**Holistic education** is a philosophy of education based on the premise that each person finds identity, meaning, and purpose in life through connections to the community, to the natural world, and to humanitarian values such as compassion and peace. Holistic education aims to call forth from people an intrinsic reverence for life and a passionate love of learning" (Ron Miller).

Robin Ann Martin (2003) describes this further by stating, "At its most general level, what distinguishes holistic education from other forms of education are its goals, its attention to experiential learning, and the significance that it places on relationships and primary human values within the learning environment." Our goals in education are each student's individual happiness, the development of their unique identity, the cultivation of personal talents and interests, and attention to the inner world as a primary source of infinite potential and growth. Our goal is to establish the strength of the individual with the elements of creativity, connectivity, natural curiosity, self-expression, clear communication, and centered, self-aware consciousness so that each student can thrive in the rapidly changing world.

At The Element School we embrace the philosophy of integrated education, a holistic way of thinking, learning, and living that encompasses multiple layers of meaning and experience rather than approaching learning as a study of disparate subjects. We also value **arts integration** as a means to increase appreciation and understanding of the wealth of knowledge in general subject areas while fostering student engagement, imagination, aesthetic sense, personal self-expression, creative and independent thinking, problem solving, decision-making, and promoting self-confidence and personal growth. We apply the **theory of multiple intelligences** with the understanding that each child possesses all modes of intelligences, and these modes serve as resources in various fields of inquiry and at various times of the day. We acknowledge the use of these various modes of intelligence not as another label to place on the child but as a means to expand avenues of learning by approaching subjects and new information from a variety of approaches. New knowledge may be assimilated through movement, visual expression, speech, music, self-reflection, or through interaction with others.

We view learning as an organic process, with a vitality of its own when it integrates all aspects of the learner's being: mental, emotional, spiritual, physical. The teacher's role is to provide a rich environment for learning, refreshing nutrients of inspiration, enthusiasm, and passion, and a willingness to let each child grow at her own pace with the higher goal of overall health and well-being and the development of personal strengths and resilience. As Carl Jung states, "one looks back with appreciation to the brilliant teachers, but with gratitude to those who touched our human feelings. The curriculum is so much necessary raw material, but warmth is the vital element for the growing plant and for the soul of the child."

To hear more about the philosophy behind The Element School, watch a video interview with Founder Enicia Fisher on The Element School's YouTube Channel: **https://www.youtube.com/watch?v=kEU3HUMrJBE**

A Little Child Shall Lead Them
By Dr. Deborah McGill

"And a little child shall lead them." They say we are in the shifts of the ages. I believe it to be true. The times and energies are upon us as we find the old ways no longer seem to be working. We find our emotions stirring, our bodies feeling pain from past emotional or nutritional wounds, our relationships being challenged or falling apart, various circumstances arising from the past that need processing, and plainly... our lives are in a flux of unfinished business. We are looking for the "corrective emotional experience" of childhood wounds. How can we correct this dynamic for the next generations?

Education is in its new paradigm and Imagine Wisdom Education, known as I-WE, recognizes every child as a wise and divine being. In this way we teach them to have "internal validation" in lieu of "external validation." My prayer is our children and grandchildren will no longer look outside themselves for their answers, they will find them from within. The "inner child" work is what we as adults do to bring us current to be in the here and now and reclaim our vitality. As we educate our children in a new and integrative way, we hold space within the Field which helps nurture what they were born with, their Essence. As adults, we talk about going with the flow, about letting go, about trusting the process, and about "being still and know that I am God." We encourage each other to stay in our Hearts and keep our childlike authenticity. These challenges are what we are shifting with Love and Awareness as our keys. The beauty of change is chaos and is needed to create the dancing Star.

A quote I have loved, "You so often experience change as though something terrible were happening, when in reality the change is moving you from confinement into Freedom, from habit into Truth."
~ Emmanuel

I was an educator and school principal for many years. I left that career in 1994 as my life got turned inside out and upside down. I lost everything I once knew and when I resurfaced from the depth of bewilderment, I went back to school to get a second Master's Degree in Clinical Psychology with an emphasis on Marriage and Family Therapy. I wanted to know what happened to me, to my life, and to my children who were now grown and beginning a life of their own. With a deep passion for the phenomenological aspect of human intimacy, I entered a doctorate program. Finishing up my Psy.D. in 2000, I was feeling quite accomplished. However, in 2004, my world once again got turned upside down and inside out as I left my traditional psychotherapy practice and was called to Ubud, Bali for *The Quest for Global Healing Conference* with Desmond Tutu. I have learned when Spirit moves, I pay attention. :)

After returning to the states a month later, I knew I could not go back to traditional therapy. There is so much more available to us than the "traditional" system or structures that so many of us learned. So, the past decade has been filled with a Pilgrimage to Ireland, Esoteric studies, Sacred Sites, Archetypes, Numerology, I-Ching, Astrology, and a whole lot of Energy and Chakra System learning along with Crystals and Zero Point Field, etc. You see, I LOVE learning, I love knowing what it truly means when I say... "As above. So below. As within. So without."

My world today is one of a Wounded Healer who has found meaning in her life from "both sides of the couch." I have discovered the examined life is one worth living. :) I am blessed to co-facilitate Emotional Healing workshops at Esalen Institute in which I have learned much. Esalen became a very big part of my Spiritual Journey. I began to participate in experiential workshops starting in 1997. During this time I had a dream to one day teach there. My dream came true beginning 2001 and since that time I co-facilitate twice a year with a beautiful partner, Terry Hunt, a psychologist from the Boston area. My soul has been enriched through the years and there are no words to express my gratitude for my Esalen experiences. What I have learned through the years is that experience is so much more than knowledge. As I have worked with adults on Emotional Healing, there has always been the questions of how did they get wounded? What happened to shut them down from their authentic self? What was the cause of their defenses that took away their vitality and essence. The answers stemmed from their experiences and education, their beliefs and values.

Esalen has a Gazebo for the children. My heart has been moved as I observed how they have integrated self trust and success. I have observed how important it is to allow the children to experience their worlds and not dictate to them as regular school systems do. As an ex-principal, through the years of my own growth, I have pondered many questions like... "How do we teach a child to live from within and own their individual personalities?" "How do we teach them to trust themselves?" "How do we allow them to stay free and happy?" "How to we teach them to trust their own instincts?"

Education, Spirituality and Psychology flow together in a Beautiful Tapestry of many colors with gold threads throughout. In the old paradigm school was to prepare us for our careers while our relationships often grew into marriages. We had children and the cycles began again, often without much thought. It was what our parents did. It is what we observed. It is what we learned. We often moved forward with an unconscious process that had been interjected through parents, culture and educational systems. However, the "new" gold threads are now emerging. So wonderful to see these new energies coming in, the new children, the new learning strategies, and the new systems and paradigms.

The process of individuation and "knowing thyself" and "to thine own Self be true" is so much more than a mere concept or thought. It is a depth of the human spirit that digs deep into the individual and collective psyche while finding the wisdom of the ages. I have heard we are moving from a 7 centered into a 9 centered being. Our DNA is changing and new information is coming in on a daily basis. Whoa! And oh so exciting! When all is said and done... this is our human journey. How blessed we are to be here at this time on planet Earth.

My passion for learning has brought me to a study of a system that came in after the harmonics convergence in 1986. It is the most complex system I have discovered yet. It is called the Human Design System. I feel it is time to step deeper into the Heart Wisdom of what this spiral journey has brought me to. I am excited to bridge my specialty of Inter-generational Psychology [where we have come from and who our ancestors were], the Wisdom of Imago [the unconscious mate selection] based on the Attachment Theory, along with all the Energy of the Chakra System.

The knowledge of the Human Design is ultimately for children, and the Children Development. It teaches the adult how to interact with children in very practical ways that nurture their development. The study of Human Design includes the dynamics of the conditioning of both children and parents, what is correct conditioning, the different types of interactions between the parent and children what conditioned parental authority is, the proper nurturing of the four types, Generator, Projector, Manifestor, and Reflector children; what the 'dysfunction' is, the profiling patterns; and aligning a child with its personality. This is essential information for the well-being and nurturing of children and their families.

Coming full circle in the cycles of Life, my Heart Wisdom brings me back to the children. They say "knowledge is the beginning of wisdom" and what I know is "our children are our future." It is time to learn new strategies to educate them on a deeper level than we have yet learned. I am honored to be a part of this new paradigm for the 21st century.

Namaste' Dr. Deb

Further information:
If you are interested in knowing more about Dr. Deb's personal counseling, life consulting, experiential workshop, dream analysis and Human Design, please contacts Deborah at any of the following:

Dr. Deborah McGill - 949.705.9137

www.facebook.com/Dr.DeborahMcGill
www.globalheartwisdom.com
www.hummingbirdtemple.com
hummingbirdtemple@gmail.com

HeartThread and Healing
By Karen Trujillo-Heffernan

Children are the natural healers of our world. Imagine a healthy newborn baby, so often the first image we see is a wide-eyed, smiling child who is emanating pure light. As children develop in the first few years they are quick to hug you, touch you and speak truth. They live from the essence of their heart.

When I first learned HeartThread: a modality facilitated with love as the thread, that releases self-doubt, unwinds old, limiting patterns held in our body and brings in self-authority, I marveled at its simplicity and effectiveness and I immediately thought of how children do this in their natural state of being.

Have you ever noticed how much better you feel after receiving a hug from a child? Or how accurate a child's simple words are? Children connect to you straight from the heart and their touch and the vibration of their voice is naturally healing. These are the principals of the HeartThread work. When we enter the world our "container", our body is pure and open to infinite love. When we grow as humans, we often forget this limitless pure essence and become burdened with limitations.

The container for the transformation of limitation is love, acceptance, constancy, presence and space. There has to be room in the body for the new to come in and the old to leave. Just understanding something mentally does not provide the space necessary for transformation, which is the objective of HeartThread.

As we grow, our body gets filled with false messages that keep us from living our fullest potential. This occurs when children are hurt by adults, bullied or invalidated and it is precisely these incidents that cause a tear in our essence. Imagine a child whose teacher puts pressure on him while standing at the chalkboard thus creating a feeling of inadequacy; a child caught in the middle of an argument between his parents and asked to take sides. A child made fun of on the playground by her peers for reading books instead of running around.

Most people have experienced situations like this as a child and we begin to doubt ourselves, perhaps lose a bit of self-confidence. Equally damaging, our self-esteem begins to be whittled away. HeartThread sessions restore our self-esteem and release the pain and false beliefs caused by such incidents.

These type of unresolved hurts, grief and disappointments are shunted to parts of our body where patterns develop that "hold" our fears and angers. These unexpressed emotions and mental ideas of reactivity become beliefs that reside within our bodies, creating places of "held" energy and dis-ease. Our breath no longer reaches the innermost parts of us, thus creating stagnation and separation in our body and within its systems.

When we are joined through the heart, we feel safe. As an organism, this sense of safety influences and affects every cell in our body. No matter what has happened to us mentally, emotionally, or physically, holding our heart with the HeartThread intention energizes all of our cells, bringing light into them, balancing them, opening them, and assisting them to flow with the energy of our consciousness.

HeartThread has proven to be very effective with children. Part of the appeal to children I have worked with, is how easy and simple the sessions are. I have utilized HeartThread with children ages 10 to 17, offering individual sessions, as well as group sessions with their parents. One 10-year-old client wrote the book, *How The Heart Works* (found on Lulu.com), following a HeartThread session.

I am passionate about bringing the HeartThread work to the world especially focusing on families and schools. I am equally passionate about bringing forth developmentally appropriate child care and education arenas for our children.

Schools and home care facilities that respect the wisdom of children by guiding and teaching to their level and to the full essence of their spirit, mind and body. Where modalities that bring balance and wholeness to a child, as well as create a safe foundation of unconditional love are a daily offering.

When children grow and learn in such arenas they will grow in the fullness of themselves and perhaps never need to utilize modalities such as HeartThread. For now, HeartThread is one of the powerful healing modalities available to restore wholeness, bring in self-authority, release self doubt and transform people so as to live in the essence of their infinite self and love.

Karen is a Mother, Family Coach, Early Childhood Professional, CA State Mentor Teacher and Energetic Lightworker.
She can be contacted at (949) 547-4066; karen4kids88@yahoo.com
www.surfinyoursoul.com

Where Giving Back comes Before Art
By Christian Lewis

Christiana Lewis, a very talented artist, left for Thailand on Feb 5, 2014 for a mission trip to do art with the orphans there. She is sharing with us the importance of Service. She was particularly generous to us, when Christofer was ill, and donated an amazing art piece to our Fundraiser. I am so grateful for her in our world.

"For the past 27 years I have been working with children and adults through the process of art. Art for many, like myself is a form of peace and therapy. Besides therapy it builds confidence, motor and technical skills as well as strengthens brain activity.

Art when it is an intentional form of "therapy," has been scientifically documented to save lives, cure the terminally ill and bring life back to people that have not spoken in years because of a tragedy.

On this journey in Thailand I will be creating confidence through the power of love in self-portrait painting. We will be exploring the many different uses of watercolors, and how to make your own watercolors and tools out of nature's natural resource from Thailand's breathing land. Turning muddy water into a lovely skin tone or brush stroke, crushing plants and flowers in water to create the most vibrant of colors, and using finger sticks and leaves to serve beautifully as paintbrushes.

We will be discussing the beauty we all possess, globally...on the exterior, but more importantly interior. No matter our skin tone, texture, scar or misshapen feature (in our eyes) we were all created unique and beautiful. The process of painting our self-portraits will release the unique beauty we all possess. No matter the style... realistic, abstract, symbolic or classic, the process will unleash a sense of self-love, laughter and confidence that is cathartic to all."

Contact: www.ChristianaFineArt.com **949.424.4077** and **goca.com**

ACKNOWLEDGEMENTS

My deepest gratitude goes to my beautiful, precious son and Angel, **Christofer**. Though his mission upon this planet was fulfilled just before his fourth birthday, Christofer walks alongside me every day, encouraging and inspiring me. In fact, he can be credited with inspiring the book, which is in your hands, and the educational model it describes. He recently expressed to me the importance of me completing the book and putting the I-WE educational model out into the world at this time; so here it is! Christofer is my greatest supporter, and I am so grateful that he chose to let me be his mother for his short time on this earth, and that he remains with me still on my journey and mission. He has been, and continues to be, the greatest blessing in my life.

DEEP GRATITUDE

There are so many beautiful people in my life who believed in this book and the I-WE model so strongly, that they jumped in to help me in so many ways to move all of this forward. I am so grateful to each of them who held my hand through crunch-time.

Jen Hutchinson: You stood by me offering your wisdom since this model was first birthed five years ago. You have been instrumental in helping me structure and complete this manuscript. Your belief in the importance of my bringing this into the world led you to squeeze time out of your own very busy schedule to help me complete this book. My gratitude goes out to you for all of this and so much more!

Ami Sattinger: Thank you for going beyond the call of duty to help me get me this out in time, helping me communicate the ideas in my head in a way that could be easily understood by readers. You did a wonderful job of helping me polish this book, and were instrumental in its completion. Thank you for your support!

Karene Cargill: My greatest acknowledgement goes to you, my dear friend. You "held my hand" in the last and final (and sometimes "wee") hours of creating this book. Your help, along with **Maia DellaCascata**, brought me into the homestretch with fewer gray hairs! Thank you both!

Mandy Gordon and Kimo Estores: Thank you Angels for stepping in the last day to take care of the first Social Media aspect of things. You complete the Production Team! And I love you both dearly!

Maura Hoffman: You are an angel in my life in so many ways. Thank you for finalizing the edits and for the help with my Toastmaster's speech. You are so amazing to me in all that you do and all that you are. I love you more than words can say!

James Frank Boswell: Thank you so much for taking over the Social Media campaign for the official book release and for converting all my contacts into a program that makes more sense. You are such a kind spirit and I am so grateful for your generous help!

Suri Phaungphakdi: Thank you dear one for stepping in and adding your beautiful energy and polishing touch to this first edition!

A special "Thank You" goes to **Deepa Somasundaram**, of the Montessori School of Laguna Beach, for supporting and contributing to the I-WE model all these years.

I would also like to thank the **Laguna Beach Community** for giving me the opportunity and privilege to work with your children, and for being co-creators of this model. The love and support I received from this Community during Christofer's illness and transition, and in the years since, is priceless! A special thanks to **Justine Amodeo** and **Suzanne De Carion** for being the first ones to believe in this vision and entrust their children in my care, as well as spreading the word to their children's friends and families.

I do not have words to adequately express the deep level of gratitude I feel in my heart for each of you who have supported this project and made it possible. I could not have done this on my own; it was truly a 'village' project, and each of you has made an important contribution in some way, even if just to encourage me. I feel tremendously blessed to have been chosen to birth this educational model into the world, but even more so to have the privilege of partnering with and being supported by such an incredible tribe! Thank you all!

It is also important to note that this model is a collaborative effort that has included many brilliant minds, teachers, friends and community leaders, in its co-creation. A special shout out to our wonderful local visionaries: **Catherine Clark, Linda Crow, Nancy Dantoni, Eddie Krajec, Susan Hough, Michelle Hutchinson, Donna Le Clair, Andrea Oyen, Andrea Riggs, Nadia Sommer, Kimberlee Schultz, Susan Tenison and KT Turner**, as well as

Juliet & Magela Ulibarri. I couldn't have done this without them! Truly, such talent and generosity there!!!

Last, but definitely not least, I want to thank my parents for bringing me into this world, my ancestors for paving the way and watching over me still, God/Goddess/All That Is, The Great Divine Creation that governs our Universe, Mother Earth Gaia, All Angels in All Dimensions that have provided their loving assistance to see this project come to world and for supporting me in being of service, for the highest good for all.

CALL TO ACTION

It has been my honor to introduce the I-We model to you.
I am happy to share my knowledge and experience with you further.

Email to schedule a complementary twenty minute consultation.
I have a sliding scale fitting all needs after consultation.

contact: satyanna@me.com

🌐 Sign up for the **newsletter** &
you will be able to download these books:

Parental Reflections

A Parents Guide to Medicine Safety

ADHD Transcription

http://imaginewisdomeducation-iwe.com

👍 LIKE the page on **Facebook** &
you will be able to download these books:

How Brain-Friendly Learning Can Release
Your Childs Infinite Potential

101 Romantic Ideas

https://www.facebook.com/ImagineWisdomEducation

If you want to know more about the I-WE Model:
Please visit the website http://www.imaginewisdomeducation-iwe.org/

Thank You So Much! ☺

CELEBRATING YOU!

AND…

Celebrating the I-WE model

Spreading its Wings

With Deep Gratitude!

NOTE FROM THE AUTHOR

In an effort to complete this project in time for our 5th Annual Green Valentines Festival, Celebrating our Youth and Sustainable Living, I utilized our community for the editing process. My sweet sisters stepped in at the last minute and worked countless hours in an attempt to deliver some level of excellence.

This is a labor of love intended to inform and inspire, rather than evoke any judgment about imperfections. So, while some may catch a few errors that were overlooked, I invite you to practice forgiveness, and ask yourself how these judgments and opinions are serving you in your own personal life.

Are they giving you 'Analysis Paralysis,' as it does to so many? Mediocrity is a natural part of human instinct to 'fit in' and is one of the elements that keeps most of us playing small, hiding under some disguise of needing to do things perfectly, or to be like everyone else, so not to stand out alone.

If you find any of the spelling, punctuation, or other formatting issues to be distracting in its imperfection, I invite you to volunteer to be an editor on my next project. It truly takes a village!

Honestly, in our model, spelling, while important, is not a primary focus. While we teach reading and writing early on, we do so to enable children to read and write as they desire. If we had strived for perfection, instead of excellence, this booklet may not be in your hands today.

We know that while there are some children who thrive at Spelling Bees, most of us can still communicate very effectively without mastering that skill. And, as it outlines later in this book, some of the greatest leaders of our world have been labeled as dyslexic and/or learning disabled.

We acknowledge and applaud all learning styles and abilities in our children and adults. We celebrate children who dare to be great, take chances and are willing to dare to write in their journals, in community papers, or in essays.

Modern technology has blessed the world with Spell Check, yet even Spellcheck is not perfect, yet! Instead of Striving for Perfection, Strive for Excellence!

"Striving for perfection is the greatest stopper there is.

It's your excuse to yourself for not doing anything.

Instead, strive for excellence, doing your best."

-Sir Laurence Oliver

THE CHILDREN OF THE FUTURE THANK YOU!

I would love to share my first speech with you about this work so dear to my heart. I offer it with Love, Inspiration and Gratitude as we all continue on our paths to making the world a better, brighter place and following our dreams ☺

Once upon a time the animals had a school. They created a curriculum to satisfy everyone with four subjects: Running, Climbing, Flying and Swimming. To be fair, all the animals had to study all subjects.

The duck got an A+ at swimming, passed flying and running, but totally flunked climbing. So they made him drop swimming to stay after school and practice climbing. This was kept up until his webbed feet were badly worn and he was only average at swimming. But average is acceptable in school so nobody worried about it much, except the duck.

The Eagle was considered a troublemaker. In the climbing class, he beat all the others to the top of the tree, but was punished for not following the rules and had to write 500 times "Cheating is wrong!"

The zebra played hooky a lot because the ponies made fun of his stripes, and he felt sad.

The fish came home and said, "Mom, Dad, I hate school. Swimming is great. Flying is fun when they let me start in the water. But running and climbing? I don't even have legs; and I can't breathe out of the water."

Like many, I believe that there are fundamental flaws in our public education system.

We need to let the fish swim, the monkey climb and the eagles fly.

We don't want the children of the future to turn into average ducks!

As a teacher, I have reviewed countless educational studies and statistics. Sadly, only 2 out of 7 children thrive within the public education system, leaving many students feeling somewhat inadequate and a few suffering greatly. There are many contributing factors to this tragic situation, but one of the greatest is the lack of consideration for the varied ways children learn.

Guess what these people have in common: Albert Einstein, John Lennon, Sir Richard Branson, Leonardo Da Vinci, Walt Disney and John Kennedy?

Yes, they all made a mark in the world, however, these outstanding people were labeled dyslexic and made to feel dumb in school. Not surprisingly, they were all men. ☺ Boys are 2 to 3 times more likely to suffer from dyslexia because they tend to use one side of their brain for language tasks, whereas girls use both hemispheres.

It is also interesting to note that two powerful forces in life such as Love **and** Money; or Relationships/Communication/Connection and Survival or Financial Literacy, are **not at all** the focus of our primary education.

5 years ago, my precious child, Christofer, was diagnosed with an inoperable brain tumor and transitioned just before his 4th birthday. He has been and continues to be my greatest teacher. Because I can no longer mother him, my Angel Christofer, has inspired me to continue sharing my motherly love with the Children of the World. He is guiding me to spread an innovative and international educational model called I-WE, Imagine Wisdom Education.

At I-WE, Love is the foundation with Imagination as the Inspiration. Because of the small study groups, this multi-intelligence focused model addresses each child's needs, as they arise. Many of our teachers are community leaders who share their passions with the children, helping them to discover their unique gifts and share them with the world through early apprenticeships. It has been said and we agree: Children learn best when they are known, explore their passions and engage all of their senses.

Once one can read, one can teach oneself just about anything. Thus, we take great care to teach reading and writing in a fun way, during the preschool years, along with foreign languages. According to Maria Montessori, the founder of Montessori Education, children are like sponges that absorb everything in their environment until the age of 6. Our public education system doesn't even start before the age of 5, missing this amazing window of opportunity for effortless learning.

Now, if you would take a deep breath with me, and some may want to close your eyes... Imagine you are in a beautiful place in nature, there are animals nearby, children of all ages are digging in the dirt, laughing. They study biology while planting seeds, learning communication skills while picking fresh vegetables from the garden for lunch. An elder in a circle is teaching history through story telling, kids exercise doing yoga, while others rehearse for a musical play, learning mathematics by dancing and playing instruments. Another group is constructing a large tree house as their architectural and interior design project, using sacred geometry ornaments. So many gifts come from working together as a team to co-create shared visions. Can you imagine a child you love, learning this way? You may open your eyes...

According to the Dalai Lama, "*Compassion is the missing ingredient in public schools and the key element that will enable children to clean up the mess we left for them.***"** At I-WE, compassionate communication is a daily practice along with conscious breathing.

We need leaders at this time who are self-actualized and care for the highest good of all beings, with entrepreneurial minds and strong values.
Many believe as we do, that life is lived *Inside-Out*. I repeat Inside/Out!
Like Gandhi said: Peace Begins With Me - And each one of YOU!

YOU can make a difference. You can use our principals to enrich the lives of the children around you. Or, you can create your own I-WE community altogether.

My greatest joy is to offer guidance and support those desiring to expand our I-WE communities around the world.

To recap, we know that the public education system is failing many of our children who are left feeling inadequate, and some even suffering. *I-WE* is an evolutionary, community based, educational model designed to prepare students for global living and peaceful leadership.

If you agree that the children deserve a better future, I invite you to be a catalyst for change. Visit our Website, Follow us on Facebook and share the I-WE principles with your family and friends. The Children of the Future WILL thank YOU!

PS: The story in the beginning was borrowed for my speech, to illustrate our point, but, it is authored by George H. Reavis and titled: Animal School ☺ So grateful for this great interpretation!

His whole book is available on Amazon:

http://www.amazon.com/The-Animal-School-George-Reavis/dp/1884548318

THIS BOOK WAS INSPIRED BY, AND DEDICATED TO OUR ANGEL: CHRISTOFER!

Here are some of the messages that

Our Angel left for us all:

"Have Fun"

"Be Happy"

"Love and Help each other more"

"BE REAL"

Christofer

My Angel Christofer is holding my world up and directing me from the other side of the veil. This book was put together, from beginning to end, in six weeks.

THANK YOU CHRISTOFER FOR HOLDING ME UP AND SHINING YOUR LIGHT ON MY LIFE, AND FOR THE CHILDREN OF THE WORLD.

ABOUT THE AUTHOR

SATYANNA CHRIS LUKEN

**Montessori, French and Yoga Teacher
Photographer,
Green Valentines Festival Founder
Author of** *ABC of Conscious Parenting - Agreements Before
(and after) Conceiving*

Satyanna Chris Luken, (also known as Anna Krajec) was born and raised in France. She is the Visionary behind I-WE and the founder of Green Valentines Festivals, which were both created to raise awareness of sustainable living and aimed at creating a bright future for our children.

Satyanna was trained in the Montessori school system seventeen years ago and taught seven years at Anneliese's Academy, a Waldorf inspired, multi-intelligence focus school. She brings many other skills to the table: twenty years of teaching, extensive world travel, and working with teens and people of all ages, in the fields of yoga, meditation and personal growth.

Her book, *ABC of Conscious Parenting, Agreements Before (and after) Conceiving*, was inspired by her son Christofer, whom she lost to a brain tumor nearly six years ago, just before his fourth birthday. The book is available on Amazon or as an e-book from her website, http://www.ABCofConsciousParenting.com.

That book is endorsed by Marianne Williamson (*Congressional candidate, spiritual activist, lecturer, and founder of Peace Alliance and Project Angel Food, and author of four best-selling books*) and Steven Farmer (award-winning author of *Children's Spirit Animal Stories and Cards*.

In 2010, Satyanna taught an eight-year-old autistic boy for eight months and was instrumental in his ability to learn, connect with other children, and find a sense of overall peace. She has now worked other special needs children who are still thriving with the I-WE model.

Satyanna is committed to connecting, inspiring, and empowering young people. Her vision is to create communities around the world of youth ages 2-27 where the younger children have role models to learn from while the older ones have a chance to develop life-long leadership skills. Elders come to share their wisdom with the youth and vice-versa.

Love is her inspiration and she has held this vision of a new education system for our youth for many years. Finally she has connected with and gathered these amazing community leaders, willing to share their passion and skills with our youth.

www.ingramcontent.com/pod-product-compliance
Lightning Source LLC
Chambersburg PA
CBHW041432300426
44117CB00001B/4